WRITE YOUR YEAR

365 WAYS TO CHANGE YOUR YEAR AND YOUR LIFE

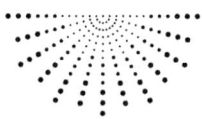

JESSICA GRACE COLEMAN

Published by Flip The Script Travel Transformation Services
Stafford, UK.

Print Edition April 2021
ISBN 9798737365479

Copyright © Jessica Grace Coleman 2021

Jessica Grace Coleman asserts the moral right to be identified as the author of this work. All rights reserved in all media. No part of this publication may be reproduced, stored in a retrieval system, or transmitted, in any form, or by any means, electronic, mechanical, photocopying, recording or otherwise, without the prior written permission of the author and/or publisher.

This book is dedicated to the dreamers, but also to the action takers, who are on a constant mission to change their lives for the better.

You've got this!

CONTENTS

Free Planner   vii

Introduction   1
Your Daily Prompts   5
Conclusion   275

About The Author   277
Other Books by Jessica Grace Coleman   281
Connect With Jess   283
Join Our Insta Challenge   285
Intro to Write Your Life   287

FREE PLANNER

As a thank you for buying this book, I've put together a free Write Your Year downloadable planner to use in conjunction with the prompts in *Write Your Year: 365 Ways To Change Your Year And Your Life*.

You can find the planner over at www.jessicagracecoleman.com/planner.

Happy planning!

INTRODUCTION

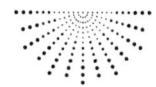

Welcome to *Write Your Year: 365 Ways To Change Your Life*, a companion book to *Write Your Life: The Ultimate Life Hack For Achieving Your Dreams*.

In *Write Your Life*, I showed you how you can use fun creative writing exercises to come to terms with your past, fully appreciate your present, and set goals and ambitions for the future that will completely change your life. In the book I also told stories from my own life, showing you exactly how to put these exercises into practice using the Write Your Life Method.

This book is a little different. Basically, I'm going to give you – as the title suggests – 365 ways to change your life over the next year, in the form of one prompt per day. As with everything related to the Write Your Life Method, most prompts will – in some way or other – relate to writing or the power of words, but don't worry: I'm not going to give you a creative writing exercise every day.

Some prompts, for example, will rely on you simply writing something down, as if you were writing a journal, or creating a message to send to someone. Some will look at the power of self-talk and mantras, while others will involve exercises that show us the power words and writing have on ourselves and others.

Hint – it's not just about changing yourself to change your life; often, we can only change our lives when we first change (improve) the lives of others. These prompts are designed to make you rethink your life, to help you appreciate what really matters in life, and to show you that helping others can completely change the way you think, act, and give. (As with *Write Your Life*, 10% of the profits of this book will go to Dolly Parton's Imagination Library, which sends free books to kids all over the world).

Writing can help you solve all kinds of problems, such as issues you're having at work, arguments you keep having with your spouse, or life decisions you need to make about your career, your partner, or where you live. Even just the act of putting your problems into words can help you see things from a different perspective, and this works for the good things in your life too.

These prompts will not change your life instantly; the cumulative effect of doing one of these prompts a day (or even just a few a week if you're busy) will help you transform your mindset, your attitude, and your perspective, which in turn will allow you to plan your goals and go after your dreams.

On each page you'll find a prompt for the day, as well as some ideas to help you get going, and (where needed) some alternatives if you can't/don't want to do the suggested prompt. Some of these will seem scary to some people, so feel free to skip any you really don't want to do, but please keep in mind that we won't achieve anything wonderful in life if we never step outside our comfort zones. The old phrase 'do one thing a day that scares you' can really help when it comes to self-development and personal growth – within reason, of course!

Some days the prompts won't be applicable, and that's OK. Just make a note of any you don't do and then complete these prompts on a future day – when your situation is more suited to doing them – before going on to the next day's prompt instead. Some of the prompts will involve you getting outside your comfort zone, and the more you do this, the easier it will become (and the richer your life will become for it!).

You can start this book at whichever point in the year you like, but please do one thing for me before you begin: make a note in your diary or calendar of the date you're starting this book. Then, scroll ahead and make another note a year from now, stating that it's been 365 days since you began reading this book. If you commit to *Write Your Year* and complete the majority of the prompts written in these pages, you should find that in 12 months' time, you'll have changed your mindset, your goals, and – hopefully – the way you live your life.

I encourage you to keep a (brief) daily diary, detailing any of the prompts you try and any good things that come from doing them.

You can also keep track of your progress on social media, posting about the prompts you complete and any wins you get from them. Just use the hashtag #writeyouryearpromptbook and tag @traveltransformationcoach on Instagram. If you do, I'll give you a shout-out!

One more thing I highly recommend, as this will come in handy once you've finished the book: bookmark any prompts you find particularly fun, interesting, insightful, or useful, as well as any that yield good results for you. Just bookmark the pages on your device or make a note of the page numbers somewhere as you read through the book.

You can find out more about how to make the most of this book by downloading the completely free Write Your Year Planner, available now at www.jessicagracecoleman.com/planner.

So, are you ready to Write Your Year? All it takes is one turn of the page...

YOUR DAILY PROMPTS

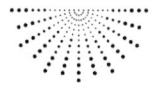

1.

Write a journal entry, describing exactly how you feel in this moment. Ask yourself the following questions:

- Are you happy right now?

- Do you long for more? If so, what?

- What's the biggest issue or most pressing concern in your life right now?

- What do you wish you could change about yourself?

- If you had the finances and resources to do so, what would you change about your life? Your job? Your house? Your relationship? Your fitness? Your health?

- What one word would you use to describe your emotional state in this moment?

Be as honest as possible; you don't have to show this to anyone else. If you're feeling sad, lonely, helpless, or lost, say so – but, more importantly, make sure you write it down. Writing things down is so much more effective than just thinking things and then immediately forgetting them. Write them down. Make the words stick. Read through your answers again.

Then, keeping the words you've written in mind, ask yourself: are you ready to take the next step towards changing your life?

2.

Take a moment to sit and think of everything you're grateful for today – and then write them down. These can be as general or as specific as you like, such as:

- My warm, cosy house

- The family dog, who's always so happy to see me

- The fact that I have enough money for all the basics: food, clothes, shelter, electricity, water

- The great book I've been reading

- My wonderful friends and the Zoom call we just had

- My family

- Chocolate, chocolate, chocolate!

This is a great practice to do every day, although – for now – just one day will do. The more we pause and think about all the wonderful things we have in our lives, the more we find ourselves being grateful for the little things, things we usually don't even give a second thought.

In general, truly grateful people are happier and have more positive mindsets.

3.

Come up with your own personal daily mantra – a few words or sentences you can say to yourself every morning, as soon as you wake up. And don't worry – you can say them to yourself in your head, so they can be as cheesy as you like. Here are some examples:

• I am awesome and can achieve anything I set my mind to.

• It's a brand new day full of brand new opportunities, and I'm going to kick some ass!

• I am healthy and happy and have everything I need, right now, to go after my dreams.

• I am grateful for everything I have in my life and for everything I get to achieve today.

• I'm going to get so much done today, and nothing and no one's going to get in my way!

• I am grateful for everything I have in my life, and I can achieve anything I set my mind to.

This may seem a little silly to some people, but keep an open mind. Self-talk – the things we say to ourselves on a regular basis – is so important, as it really can affect the way we see ourselves and the way we treat ourselves. Stop telling yourself you're dumb, or stupid, or that you can't do something or that you don't have any willpower or that you're never going to be as successful as you'd like to be.

Instead, tell yourself you're awesome, and that you deserve all the success and love in the world. How we talk to – and about – ourselves matters, so swap that negative self-talk for some words of affirmation.

4.

Spend a few minutes reading some inspirational and/or motivational quotes on the internet. Quotes like:

"The most difficult thing is the decision to act. The rest is merely tenacity" – Amelia Earhart

"A surplus of effort could overcome a deficit of confidence" – Sonia Sotomayor

"You just can't beat the person who never gives up" – Babe Ruth

I know, I know, motivational quotes can seem a little cheesy, but they work. There's a reason I included one at the start of every chapter in my *Write Your Life* book. They can change your mindset in an instant, can help you look at problems from a different angle, and can remind you that other people have gone through similar struggles to the ones you're facing – and come out the other side. Go one step further and print them out or write them down in a journal. You can even make this into a daily practice, finding one quote per day that really speaks to you and thinking about how you can apply it to your own life.

5.

Write a message – or letter – to someone in your life who you really appreciate. It doesn't have to be long, and you don't even have to send it if you don't want to, just get it written. Tell that person why they're so awesome, how they've impacted your life, and how grateful you are to have them in your life. It can be your partner, a friend, a family member, a colleague, even someone online you've never met (like a celebrity you admire, or someone whose book, podcast, or blog really helped you out).

As I said, you don't have to send it to them if you don't want – sometimes, just the act of writing things out, and appreciating how someone else has helped you, is enough to shift your mood and mindset – but I recommend sending it if you can. This might mean coming out of your comfort zone, which is always a good thing; how can we expect ourselves to grow as people if we never do things that make us nervous? Besides, it will no doubt give both you and the recipient of your message a boost. People often forget to tell (or don't feel comfortable telling) people how much they mean to them, and one day, it's going to be too late. Go on – write someone a nice message and really make their day.

6.

Reframe your mindset around: being healthy.

We all know what we need to do in order to keep healthy: eat nutritious food, drink lots of water, do regular exercise, look after our physical and mental wellbeing, and so on. But how many of us actually do all of that?

For many of us, staying healthy sounds like a lot of hard work, and no fun at all, but what if we changed our mindset around it?

Instead of focusing on the food we should or shouldn't be eating, the exercise we should be doing, and so on, focus on *why* we're doing it.

- Don't you want to have a long, happy life?

- Don't you want to be able to go out and do fun stuff, without getting tired?

- Don't you want to be full of energy, ready to take on the world?

- Don't you want to have the stamina to keep going until you achieve your dreams?

- Don't you want to live a full, exciting life?

Being healthy and fit will allow you to do all these things, so focus on *why* you're doing the things required to stay healthy rather than on the things themselves.

Personally, I know I wouldn't be able to do all the work required to keep my business going if I were really unhealthy, constantly eating rubbish food and never doing any exercise. How about you?

7.

Purchase a book on mindset/self-development/personal growth and plan to read at least ten minutes a day (more if you have the time), preferably in the morning.

Filling your head with positive, inspirational words and stories will motivate you to take on the day ahead with a spring in your step and a twinkle in your eye. Here are a few book options to get you started:

- *Everything is Figureoutable* – Marie Forleo
- *A Tribe Called Bliss* – Lori Harder
- *You Are A Badass* – Jen Sincero
- *The Big Leap* – Gay Hendricks
- *The Alchemist* – Paulo Coelho

The first thing we do in the morning sets our mood for the rest of the day. Waking up and immediately looking at the news – or scrolling through Instagram and getting sucked into a social media hole – can make us feel sad, helpless, or annoyed. Starting with a few pages of an inspirational, motivational book can make us feel happy, confident, and ready to own the day. I know which way I'd rather wake up.

8.

Make a list of things you can do to simplify your life. We all have so much going on – with so many balls to constantly juggle – that it never really occurs to us to pause, reflect, and think about how we can simplify our life. Even if it's just one thing, write it down and commit to doing it. For instance:

- Is there a job on your to-do list that's been there forever? Would it be the end of the world if you just put a line through it and forgot it? After all, you've gone this long without doing it…

- Can you delegate something – anything – to someone else, to give yourself a little more time?

- Do you really need to spend hours on social media, or on your phone in general? What would happen if you just put it away for a day?

- Is your home cluttered? Is it driving you mad? Don't tackle it all at once; just throw out/donate one thing a day. After a year, that's 365 fewer items cluttering up your home.

There are so many ways we can simplify our lives, and when we do, we give ourselves more time to reflect, more time to relax, and more time to plan – and go after – our goals. Go on, give it a go!

9.

Why not get a pen pal? And I don't mean someone you write online messages to or someone whose DMs you slide into occasionally; I mean a real, bonafide, ye olde type pen pal.

Yes, these still exist, and getting into the habit of writing out – on paper, no less – everything that's going on in your life can be a form of creative therapy.

You can find pen pal groups on Facebook and other websites, so just do a bit of searching. And try to get pen pals from other countries – this will definitely help you expand your horizons and see life from different perspectives.

There's just something about sitting down at a desk with a nice pen and nice writing paper and penning a letter to someone on the other side of the world – not to mention the excitement when you get a reply in the post, delivered by an actual postman! Receiving things in the post that aren't bills or takeout menus can be quite thrilling (or am I just a bit sad? Who cares).

10.

Write a speech about your special talents. That's right – I want you to sit down and write out an actual speech. It doesn't have to be long, and you don't have to actually perform it, just as long as it makes you think about your own skills and abilities.

We often lose sight of the things we're good at, so reminding ourselves of these things – and imagining how we'd present them to others, such as if we were giving a TED Talk – can be a real eye-opener.

You can do this exercise for all kinds of speeches, too. Write a speech about how you're setting goals and kicking ass, about how you're changing your life, about how you're designing your dream life – and how you're going to make it happen. Write words that are inspirational, motivational, and just plain awesome. You never know, you might inspire yourself into action.

11.

Warning: this one is a bit morbid, but it does get you thinking.

Grab a pen and paper and write down one short sentence about yourself, something that encapsulates you as a person, the way you'd want to be remembered.

Yes, that's right, I'm asking you to write what you'd want putting on your tombstone. Your eternal epitaph.

So, what is most important to you? And what do you want to be remembered for? Here are some ideas:

- Loving wife, daughter, and mother
- Loved by all
- Devoted to his family
- The epitome of grace and generosity
- She saved the world. A lot. (Okay, so that one was from *Buffy The Vampire Slayer*).

Once you've done this, ask yourself: Are you living up to this sentence? Would these immortal words be true if – God forbid – you died today? Or do you need to make some changes in your life while you still can? This is scary stuff, and it's meant to be. Life is short, so start making those changes right now!

12.

Have a Deep and Meaningful (or D&M) with someone – an emotional conversation that actually means something.

This can be difficult, I know, so first, write out a paragraph or two describing what's on your mind and what you'd like to talk about. You can always send this piece of writing to your intended D&M participant to get the conversation started if you find it hard to put your emotions into words.

In today's world, so many of our conversations consist of sending memes, asking how the other person is but only really looking for a 'Good thanks, how are you?' in response, or just talking about surface-level stuff. We might occasionally get a little deeper, but a lot of us never get *that* deep. Making these kinds of connections with people can change your mindset and your perspective, and isn't that what most of us are craving anyway? Connection?

13.

Try the following writing exercise: Write out one fear or concern you have about yourself and your life – for instance, you think you're not smart enough to start a side hustle, or you think you have nothing to say that people would be interested in, or you don't think you use your spare time wisely enough.

Then, write out one reason (or more, if you can come up with them) why this fear is untrue, unfounded, and just plain rubbish. Think about it properly and give actual 'evidence'. For example:

• Fear: I have nothing interesting to say and don't add value to anyone.

- Evidence that this is untrue: I gave advice to a friend last week about their job/career path and they said it really helped them.

- Fear: I don't get enough done in my spare time.

- Evidence that this is untrue: I get plenty done, and even if I don't, that's OK. Sometimes, resting and recharging my batteries is exactly what I need to do so I can face the new day feeling refreshed and positive.

These types of exercises are used in CBT (Cognitive Behavioural Therapy) and are designed to help you change the way you think about yourself. So, give it a go, but don't just do it once – do it every time a horrible negative thought rears its ugly head. You'll soon start to see your own awesome self in a much better, more positive light.

14.

Reframe your mindset around: judgement.

We all judge people at some time or other. We don't mean to do it, but sometimes we just can't help it. I'm sure you've judged people based on appearance – he's wearing a tweed jacket and a monocle, he must be rich/eccentric/intellectual – or based on their actions, such as when someone litters or hogs the middle lane of the motorway.

So, knowing this, why do we take it so personally when someone judges us? Our actions? Our lifestyle? Our lives? It can sting, sure, and – depending on the judgement – it can be downright painful, but it can also be relatively easy to change our thinking about being judged.

If someone judges us for something – say, an action – it often says more about them than it does about us. They might have insecurities, or limiting beliefs, or a story they tell themselves about how people should look, behave, and live their lives. None of that has anything to do with you; it's all them.

So why should we take it personally? And why should we feel bad? We shouldn't (unless, of course, we're doing something we *know* is bad, like the littering thing. Then the judgement is deserved). That person probably judges lots of people for lots of different things, but the reason they do it is inside themselves, and that's none of our concern.

When we change the way we feel about judgement, it can be truly freeing, and it works for other similar things too: when someone is mean to you, when they're jealous, when they say bad things behind your back… it all says way more about them than it does about you. In all probability, it has nothing to do with you at all.

15.

Watch one less TV show today (or read one less chapter of that novel, or spend 30 minutes less scrolling through social media) and, instead, sit down and write your own story.

Do some journalling, make a to-do list, come up with some more goals, do some creative writing to stimulate your mind… just put pen to paper and give yourself half an hour or so of just focusing on you and your life, without any interruptions from the TV, the internet, or anything else.

If it's actually impossible for you not to be interrupted for 30 minutes, do it for 10 minutes, or five minutes. Just take whatever time you can to sit and focus on yourself for a while, using writing as the medium through which you can reflect on your past and plan for your future.

16.

Join a local group (whether in 'real life' or online) to do with your interests.

Surrounding yourself with like-minded people can really give you a boost, as can either sharing your love of an existing hobby or starting a new one.

There are loads of groups out there: sports clubs, book clubs, hiking groups, quiz night groups, cooking clubs, groups who just like to meet up down the pub... the list is endless.

I used meetup.com to join a local book club, and we meet up every month either in person or over Zoom. Not only has this allowed me to meet more like-minded local people I would otherwise have never got to know, but it's also given me the chance to read a wide variety of books I wouldn't otherwise have chosen to read, expanding my horizons on many levels. And the good news is, there are all kinds of clubs and groups out there, so there's bound to be something for everyone.

17.

Make a donation to a charity that is close to your heart. It doesn't have to be much – a fiver here, a tenner there – and it doesn't have to be a major charity. Just give, and remind yourself how good it feels to give.

These days, giving to a charity – or to someone in need, such as through gofundme.com – is easier than ever before. You can just go to their website, put in your card details or sign in to Paypal, and give a one-time donation of whatever you want.

18.

Write a poem.

Write about your day, how you're feeling, or something you're looking forward to. It's all about getting those creative juices flowing and trying something a little different.

Poems can be as short or as long as you like, and you don't have to show it to anyone if you don't want to (though if you're proud of it, go ahead! Why not?). You never know, you might like it, and you might even make it a regular part of your day or week.

19.

Take a walk. Getting fresh air is so important, and changing your state can really get your thoughts flowing if you find yourself stuck on a certain issue or problem.

It doesn't matter too much where you walk, but if you can surround yourself with nature, even better. Sometimes we just need to turn off our phones and other electronic devices and reconnect with good old Mother Earth (though I also recommend walking while listening to an inspiring podcast or some uplifting/relaxing music).

Walking is so important for both our mental and physical health, especially if you have a job where you're stuck inside all day, sitting at a desk. Get those muscles moving and get that blood pumping! And don't forget to take a moment to really appreciate all that lovely fresh air you're able to breathe in.

20.

Watch a TED Talk. You can learn so much about so many different subjects through TED Talks, and many of them are insightful, inspiring, and motivational.

They're usually less than 20 minutes long, too, so you can fit one in while you're getting ready in the morning or when you're cooking dinner.

I love TED Talks, and I've watched so many of them I can't even begin to list them all. If you're unsure where to begin, head to ted.com and click on the subjects that interest you; you'll then be given some recommendations. You can also Google things like 'most watched TED Talks' to get you started.

21.

Go one day without reading or seeing any news. Actively avoid it. Instead, make sure you only read/see/listen to positive things.

This might be easy for some people and incredibly difficult for others. I understand that it's good to be aware of what's going on in the world – whether it's good or bad – but one day off won't hurt. I'm sure that if there were a zombie apocalypse you'd know about it soon enough, or one of your friends or family members would message you about it. Just give yourself a break from all the wars, epidemics, pandemics, politics, deaths, crimes, and everything else our news bulletins usually cover on a daily basis. Replace it with upbeat music, positive podcasts, TV shows that make you laugh, and so on.

Do it for one day, then maybe one day a month or one day a week. Be warned: avoiding the news can get addictive!

22.

Give your time to a local charity. This is similar to the 'give to charity' prompt, but it's here to remind you that even if you don't have money to give away, you can still help – and, in many cases, time is just as valuable as money.

If you're not sure how to go about doing this, perhaps put a post on social media asking if anyone knows of any local charities you can help out. This might include fundraising, collecting or delivering food, serving people in food banks or soup kitchens, spreading the word, and so on. Helping other people is one of the best ways we can spend our time.

23.

Tame your limiting beliefs. Get out your notepad and write down one limiting belief you have about yourself. For instance, 'I'm not good at making decisions' or 'I don't deserve to earn hundreds of thousands of pounds'. Then write a list of 5-10 reasons why this belief is UNTRUE.

For instance, 'I've made many life-changing decisions that turned out well' or 'I work hard and have worked hard for years and years; I deserve something in return'. Come back and add to the list/re-read your answers every time you feel this negative belief creeping back into your mind.

We all have limiting and negative beliefs about ourselves, but those beliefs only stick around if we keep thinking them. If, instead, we train our brains to believe the opposite, we can – slowly but surely – get rid of these bad or untrue beliefs we have about ourselves. These beliefs can be about any area of our lives: our jobs, our careers, our personal lives, our family lives, and so on.

24.

The next time you go shopping in a big store, pick up one item (or a few items) as you make your way around and put them in the charity trolley/basket on the way out of the shop (the food/items they give to local food banks and so on).

Many big supermarket chains have these baskets available, and it's so easy to simply buy a little extra something and pop it in the basket or trolley on the way out. If you do a weekly shop, perhaps make it a weekly thing, giving at least one item per week.

This is a brilliant way to give back to your local community without giving any extra effort or time, and you don't have to give large, expensive items either – even just a bag of potatoes or a few tins of soup will help give someone a hot meal, and that's a wonderful thing. I know many people who do this at Christmas, giving gifts and advent calendars for those who otherwise wouldn't receive anything over the holidays. Of course, food items are needed all throughout the year.

25.

Write your own TED Talk (see ted.com for more details).

If you WERE giving a TED Talk, what would you do it on? What would be your specialist subject? What do you already know a lot about and are super passionate about? What knowledge do you have that you want to pass on to others?

Realising what you would make a speech on can tell you a lot about what's important to you, and what's important in your life (whether you already knew it or not).

It doesn't have to be long, and I'm not saying you should go and research your subject for hours before putting pen to paper – this is all about realising what subjects you're passionate about, and what you'd choose to teach others if given the chance. Your specialist topic might surprise you, giving you ideas about a new hobby to start or a new career to pursue – you never know!

This prompt only works if you've done the previous prompt of 'watch a TED Talk', and while it's similar to the 'write a speech' prompt, for this one I want you to focus on the main point behind TED Talks: 'ideas worth spreading'.

26.

'Get better sleep' prompt: Try a soothing app or podcast to send you to sleep.

There are loads of apps to help you get to sleep. Some play soothing, relaxing music or sounds until you fall asleep (think waves crashing on the shore, rain, and so on), whereas others have people reading stories in a calm, soothing voice.

There are also plenty of podcasts aimed at sleep, and one I've used in the past – 'Sleep With Me' – just has one man rambling in a quiet, confusing manner about things many people will have no interest in. When I was listening to it, my brain got so bored and confused it just switched off and went to sleep! Remember: sleep is so incredibly important, so anything you can do to minimise distractions and help you get a better night's sleep is well worth doing.

27.

Create a playlist of some of your favourite songs from your teen years, turn up the volume, and dance around! Sing along if you remember the words, and forget about everything else going on in your life for 10-30 minutes.

This is a great activity for so many reasons. It reminds you of some of your favourite music that you might not have listened to for a while, you'll be getting in some exercise and releasing those endorphins (never a bad thing), and if you choose lively, upbeat music, it will immediately change your mindset and your mood. Just listening to upbeat music you love can help, but dancing to it (preferably on your own, or at least dancing as if no one's watching) takes things to a whole other level, happiness-wise.

28.

Sit down and Google the lyrics to some of your favourite songs. Then take a few moments to read and really take in the words, without listening to the actual music or thinking of the melody in your head (if at all possible).

This can give you a whole new appreciation for your favourite bands and artists, and for songwriters in general.

Of course, this only works for certain songs and genres of music. If all you listen to is dance music with no lyrics, or if your favourite song is something with hardly any lyrics at all, it's probably not going to work, and it might not be as profound an experience!

29.

Watch Shia LaBeouf's 'Just do it' video on YouTube.

The whole thing is pretty long, but one of the videos has been cut down to about a minute. It might be a little silly and it might make you laugh, but it's also pretty motivational.

What are you waiting for? Just do it!

30.

Try a different type of coffee or a new tea you've never had before. Go to a different coffee shop or look in a different store. Mix it up. You never know, you might find a new favourite beverage.

This is just a little thing, sure, but sometimes it's the little things that make all the difference. Our days can become so 'samey' that sometimes we just need to try something new. This can be a little overwhelming for some people, however, or just difficult to achieve if you don't have any spare time in your day to try something else. Swapping your morning drink, therefore, is quick and easy and something we can all try. Who knows? Once you change one little thing in your daily routine you might be tempted to change more, and soon you'll be out of that rut you've perhaps felt stuck in recently.

31.

Delete (or hide/ignore) one person or page on your social media feed that is too negative, that annoys you, or that makes you angry. Life is too short to listen to that negative crap.

Of course, you can delete or hide more than just one person or page – get rid of as many profiles as you need so that your feed is less full of moaning and bitching and more full of positive things.

32.

Add one person or page to your social media profile that is positive, uplifting, inspirational, and/or motivational. Fill your feed with quotes and pictures that inspire you or that simply make you feel happy.

And, again, you don't have to just stop at one. Find five or 10 new pages or people to follow and pack your feed full to the brim with positive propaganda.

33.

Change the wallpaper on your phone to something new.

If you look at your phone as much as I do, it can be a good idea to look at something new for a change, and this is your chance to put something really meaningful on there –

something that makes you smile, something that reminds you of what you're aiming for in life (or why you're striving to achieve it), or something that inspires you to go after your dreams. It's something you'll be seeing several times a day, so make it something good.

Personally, I find pictures online of dream houses I'd like to own one day, or pictures of places I've visited and want to go back to, or photos of my past holidays that I have really great memories of. I use photos that make me smile, photos that make me remember the good times, and photos of things I'm aiming for in life. If you're not utilising your phone screen, start today!

34.

Reframe your mindset around: failure.

It's one thing to know that failure is good because you learn from it and grow and know what to do (or what not to do) the next time you attempt something, but it's another thing to actually believe this to the extent that when you do fail, you don't feel devastated or upset – or embarrassed.

So, take some time to meditate on the idea of failure, and journal on it too.

Imagine yourself failing at something – at a task at work, at a job interview, or at an event or challenge, whatever it might be. Ideally, something you're striving towards right now. Would you learn anything from that failure? Would you be able to apply that lesson in the future, if you try the thing again, or perhaps apply the lesson to something completely different? Can you see how that failure would actually be a good thing in the long run?

Visualise the failure in as much detail as possible, then write down all the positive things that failure would bring you.

Visualising the failure in detail will also prepare you for if you *do* fail doing that particular task or activity in the near future.; it won't seem like such a big deal as you'll have already 'gone through it', and because you'll know that no matter what the outcome, you'll be able to use it to your advantage.

Just don't *keep* visualising the failure – we don't want to trick our brains into thinking that's what we want to happen! There's a difference between knowing how to deal with failures when they happen and actively planning to fail. We don't want to be doing the latter.

35.

Join a Facebook group (or a group on another social media platform) and introduce yourself either with a little message or a quick video. Choose something you're interested in (an existing hobby) or something you want to get into.

As adults, it can be so hard to make new friends, but fortunately, with the internet it's actually pretty easy. Joining a group of like-minded people who are interested in the same things we're interested in can help us feel like we belong, as well as expanding our social circle and our skills and knowledge. It can also be a good activity for just trying out something new and getting outside your comfort zone, which usually leads to great things.

36.

Get out your notebook and complete the following exercise, writing down your answer in as much detail as possible: If you could rewind to one time in your life (or perhaps two or three) when you felt completely happy, where would you go? And why?

Write down where you were, who you were with, what you were doing, and – most importantly – how you were feeling. Then write out a little description as if it were a scene in a novel.

Doing this exercise can be a real eye-opener. You might go back to something in your past that you haven't even thought about for years, or it might remind you of what you love doing and what makes you happy.

Is there any way you can take something from this memory and apply it to your life now? Perhaps you could reconnect with an old friend or go out and try an activity that used to make you smile. You could listen to a song you remember listening to at the time, or perhaps reevaluate your priorities based on what makes you happy. Because, if you aren't happy, the people closest to you might not be happy either. It's not selfish to make yourself and your own happiness a priority.

37.

What is the first thing you see when you wake up? An alarm clock/your phone? The wall next to your bed? A messy room? Could you change this to something more positive?

For example, if the first thing you do is turn off the alarm on your phone, use a positive, uplifting image as your phone wallpaper. Tidy your room so you're not immediately waking up to a mess, or stick a motivational image or quote (or full on vision board) next to your bed, getting your mindset right as soon as you wake up.

What we do and the things we think of first thing in the morning really do set the tone for the rest of the day. If you wake up and immediately check the news on your phone, or start scrolling through social media to see messages of people complaining, you're already putting yourself in a crappy headspace. What we 'feed' our brains with matters always, but it really matters during our first few wakeful moments of the day.

38.

Do a book swap with a friend (or a music swap, or a film swap, or anything else creative) and set a date to meet up and discuss the book/music/film.

This one's all about getting social, expanding your horizons in terms of the kind of entertainment you consume, and getting you thinking and discussing something in a way you might not be used to. Until I joined my book club, I hadn't had those kinds of discussions about books since university, and it was really great to get back into that.

39.

Treat yourself (or Treat Yo'Self, as they say in *Parks and Recreation*).

Life is short, and you deserve a treat. Go on – I'm giving you permission.

It doesn't have to be anything huge like going out and blowing a lot of money on a new car; it can be walking to the shop and buying your favourite chocolate bar, or ordering something online you've been putting off because you can't 'justify' the cost. Don't get yourself in debt over it or anything – just give yourself a little treat.

We all deserve to treat ourselves sometimes, and even little things can give us a pep in our step or give us that much-needed boost if we're feeling down. Go one better and arrange a 'treat yourself' day with a friend (again, like in *Parks and Recreation*). They have one day every year where they meet up with a friend and spend the whole day treating themselves: clothes shopping, a nice lunch, cocktails, massages, whatever makes you feel awesome. Why not arrange a treat yourself day for a date in the future? You can do that right now, and it will give you something epic to look forward to as well.

40.

Write out a story of a moment in your past when you felt embarrassed, stupid, or like everyone was laughing at you.

(Write it in the third person, like you were writing a scene in a novel).

In as much detail as you can, explain how you felt at the time, both during the event and afterwards. Then completely rewrite the scene as if you didn't feel embarrassed but instead saw the funny side, joining in with the laughter and laughing at yourself.

Sometimes, a small perspective shift is all we need.

All too often we take life far too seriously, and learning to laugh at things that happened to us in the past can help us when we come across other situations in the future in which we might feel embarrassed or like people are laughing at us. If we can laugh with them, and laugh at ourselves, life will be a whole lot easier in so many ways.

41.

Think of a negative sentence you say to yourself on a daily basis (or at least regularly). We all do it – we might think 'I'm so busy today' or 'I don't have time' or 'Why am I even bothering? I can't do this'.

Then, I want you to change this sentence into something positive, and sometimes that just means changing or adding a word or two. 'I'm so busy today' could change to 'I'm so lucky to be busy today' or 'I don't have time' could change to 'I have plenty of time to achieve all my goals'.

How we talk to ourself and the words we use matters. And, once we start changing the things we think on a daily basis, we'll be able to change how we think about ourselves and our abilities. Change your daily sentences – any negative self-talk about your abilities needs to be gone or replaced ASAP!

42.

Spend a few minutes today organising the photos on your phone or computer – deleting the ones you don't need, and perhaps putting the ones you want to keep into folders.

Organising little things encourages you to start organising your life in general, and it's always nice to go on a trip down memory lane, looking at old photos. Pay attention to the ones that make you smile or that remind you of what's important in life – this can tell you a lot about the things you should be focusing on in life, and you might remember people, places, or experiences you haven't thought about for a while.

As a content creator, my phone is always full of photos – not to mention memes and other silly things I send to my friends – so I regularly make the time to go through them all. My phone also makes little videos for me, compiling photos from certain dates or from last summer and so on and putting them together with music. This can be fun way of looking back on good times and remembering things that made you smile – things that perhaps you should bring back into your life now (if at all possible).

43.

Spring clean your house (even if it isn't spring!). Keeping your living space neat, clean, and clutter-free is so important when it comes to clearing your mind, relaxing, and having the physical and mental space to go after your dreams.

If I'm in a messy room and I'm trying to work, I just can't concentrate, and I hate unnecessary clutter with a fiery passion! Get your space sorted and your life will follow.

If this seems like too much all at once, do what I did and throw out 1-5 items a day (depending on how much extra 'stuff' you have), whether that means chucking them in the rubbish bin or putting them in a bag to donate to a charity shop. When your space is less cluttered, it's a lot easier to keep it clean and tidy.

44.

If you haven't already read Paulo Coelho's *The Alchemist: A Fable About Following Your Dream*, I highly recommend it.

It's a well-known book in the self-development sphere, and not only is it beautifully written (like Coelho's other works), but it really makes you think.

Give it a go, or at least read the excerpt on Amazon to see if it's the right kind of book for you.

45.

Ask people in your social circle what their favourite bands, artists and albums are, then pick something you've never listened to before (and preferably in a completely different genre to the ones you usually listen to) and give it a whirl. Expand your musical horizons one song at a time.

This is a great exercise as not only do you get to listen to all kinds of different genres of music that you're not used to, but you'll also learn something about your family and friends going by their recommendations and what they declare as their favourite band or favourite album. It might even help you understand them a little better.

46.

Write your Success Sentence. This is a sentence that sums up what success means to you, and it will be different for everyone.

It could mean earning so much money a year, it could mean being able to give back to your community, or it could simply mean being 'happy', whatever happiness means to you. Write it out and put it up where you'll see it on a regular basis (mine is on my vision board).

Here's mine: 'Success for me means doing what I love for a living, earning enough to live comfortably with no debt or financial stress, and having the ability to give back in a meaningful way.' And don't worry if this changes over time – as we get older and grow as people, what success means to us is actually likely to evolve and grow too.

47.

Make a list of the five people you spend the most time around – family, friends, work colleagues, and so on. Then, take each one and consider how they make you feel, whether they're aligned with your values and goals, and if they lift you up or drag you down.

We are the sum of the people we spend the most time with, and if you're surrounded by negative people who have zero goals in life, it's not going to help your mindset or your belief that you can go out there and achieve your dreams.

Is there any way you can start spending more time with more positive people, perhaps people who have similar values and goals to yourself?

This exercise can seem a little harsh, but I'm not suggesting you cut all the negative people out of your life – I'm just reminding you to be aware of how people make you feel when you're with them and, if needed, reduce the amount of time you spend with people who drain your energy (it isn't just dementors who suck hope and happiness out of people)! Then look into finding some more positive people to hang around with who will lift you up instead of dragging you down.

48.

Take a moment to sit down, take out your notepad, and come up with a character – as if you were writing a novel – of the person you really want to be.

Give them a name (or a nickname that relates to your name) and an occupation, and then describe their personality. Describe how they talk, how they walk, how they present themselves, what their values are, what their priorities are, what they've already achieved and what they're striving to achieve.

Then give them a 'costume' – an outfit that encapsulates who that person is, whether it be a power suit, fitness clothes, a retro dress and hairstyle, or whatever. This is the person you're striving to be, and it's the person you're going to become if you just keep going after your dreams.

It can also help to either draw this character or find a photo of someone on the internet who looks the part. Print it out and write down keywords describing their personality, their career, their goals etc. all around the image, then put it on your vision board (or equivalent). This is what you're aiming for, and it's absolutely achievable.

49.

Find a person or product on a site like kickstarter.com or patreon.com (or other similar sites) that you want to back financially. Just make sure it's something aligned with your goals (such as supporting another author if you're writing a book, or backing a product that will really help you with your business).

You don't have to spend a lot of money; it's all about giving back and supporting other people, just as you'd hope other people would support you if you had a new venture (which you may well have in the near future).

Through doing this, you can also learn a lot about the people, products, and services in a particular industry if you're looking to change career or start your own business. Besides, it can be nice to just be part of a community.

50.

Write your Legacy Vision. This is what you're striving for in life – the legacy you want to leave behind when you're gone.

To do this, first make a list of everything that's important to you in terms of your personal life and in terms of local and global issues. Next, answer the question: What do you want people to remember about you once you're gone?

Then, combine your answers into one solid sentence that states exactly what your legacy vision is. Put it up on your vision board or some other place where you'll see it every day to remind you what you're striving for.

Here's mine: 'To show as many people as possible how they can achieve their goals through writing and how they can design their dream life – and live it too.'

51.

Think back to what your favourite childhood book was and, if you don't own a copy, buy one (a paperback/hardback, and if possible, a really nice edition). Then read it over the next few weeks.

Hopefully, it will take you back to when you were younger and will perhaps stir up some fond memories. This can either be from when you were a child or when you were a teenager.

Two of my favourite 'childhood' books are *Anne of Green Gables* by Lucy Maud Montgomery and *The Solitaire Mystery* by Jostein Gaarder. I've just re-read *Anne of Green Gables* after picking up a lovely hardback edition, and I'm just about to re-read *The Solitaire Mystery* too. Pure nostalgia!

52.

Think back to a TV show you used to love watching as a child/teenager, and then try to find it – either on DVD or on YouTube.

We often talk fondly of shows from our pasts with friends and family, but have you ever sat down and re-watched an episode of something you used to love? Try it now – it could give you all the feels.

I had many favourite TV shows when I was a kid: *Bertha, Pigeon Street, Button Moon, The Trap Door, Postman Pan, Fireman Sam, Tube Mice...* ah, the good old days!

53.

It's time to be a badass. And, fortunately, there's a book for that – two, in fact: *You Are A Badass* and *You Are A Badass At Making Money*, both by Jen Sincero.

For today, just take a look at her website – jensincero.com – and soak in all the badassery (that's a word, right?).

Believe me, if you're feeling stuck – either with money or with life in general – these books will give you the kick up the behind you really need.

54.

Have an 'uplifting bath'. Many of us have baths to relax, and that's still the aim here, but this time have a bath while listening to a motivational podcast or uplifting music, or while reading an inspiring book, whether that be self-development or the biography of someone you admire.

Use your time in the bath to rest and recharge, but also to fill your mind with positive, uplifting messages and ideas that are going to make you feel great.

Of course, you can also do the typical 'relaxing bath' thing: surround yourself with candles, use soothing bath bombs and scented bubble bath, and have a glass of wine or something else you enjoy.

55.

Offer to be a mentor to someone.

We all need mentors in our lives, so why not give back and ask someone if they need a mentor? Think of all the skills and talents you have, then seek out someone looking to learn these things. This can be done at your job, with friends and family, or with total strangers who want to know more about a certain career or topic.

It can feel great to help someone out, and who knows? Maybe in the future they'll pay it forward and be a mentor to someone else. It doesn't have to take up all your time, either – it could just be a 30-minute Zoom call every few weeks, or answering a few texts here and there.

You can be a mentor in pretty much anything. Are you confident at giving presentations at work? I can guarantee you there are people who are not and who would love to know how to get over their fears of doing so. Are you a great writer or great at numbers? Are you a kick-ass baker or cook? Do you know how to play chess? Are you a good gardener? Do you know how to stay fit and healthy?

Once you start thinking about it, I'm sure you'll realise you have so many talents and skills that others would love to learn more about. And hey, who knows? If the mentoring goes well, maybe you could make it into a side hustle and earn some money from it!

56.

Get in touch with someone you haven't spoken to in a long time (someone you like!) and see how they're doing.

It can be great to reconnect again, and who knows? You might find someone aligned with your values and goals who is on the exact same wavelength as you. It doesn't have to be a phone call, either – send a text, or message them on social media. You never know where it might lead.

I'm sure we all have people in our lives who have disappeared from our circle or slipped through the net for whatever reason. People from school or university, people we used to work with, family members who live far away… you might even have these people as friends on social media but never talk to them. Well, why don't you give it a try today?

57.

Write a list of all the things you believe you can't do or aren't good at – things that might have stopped you from doing things in the past, such as: 'I'm terrified of speaking in public' or 'I'm never going to be fit and healthy' or 'I have a fear of driving so I'm never going to learn'.

Then, take one of them and do some research into how you could overcome this fear or limiting belief. Is there a book on the subject that could help? Is there such a thing as a coach in that area you could hire (these days, there are coaches for everything!)? Is there a YouTube video with tips on how to overcome your fear?

Pick one and do it. Read the book, watch the video, contact the coach. This is the first step towards changing your life.

So many people go through life simply managing their fears and limiting beliefs, even if it's stopping them from doing something amazing – for instance, never going on a plane because you're too scared of flying, or never being able to do a presentation at work because you're terrified of public speaking. Wouldn't it be great to overcome this fear or limiting belief? Wouldn't it feel absolutely amazing to not let that 'thing' hold you back anymore? I think so. And it just starts with one little step.

58.

Find a friend (one who won't think you're mad) and suggest a little experiment – ask if you can 'interview' each other.

This can be done in person or over video call, but either way, remember to record it. You can pretend you're on a talk show or being interviewed for a podcast or YouTube channel.

Really get deep and ask personal questions, such as: What is your number one ambition in life? What are your top three priorities? What one thing would you change about your current circumstances if you could? Who is your idol/hero? What is your best skill or talent? If you could be anywhere in the world right now, doing anything, where would you be and what would you be doing?

Go on, get deep!

As crazy as this one seems, it can have so many brilliant outcomes. You can get to know your friend better – and perhaps connect on a deeper level than you have before – and you might realise something about yourself that you've never realised before because, well, no one ever asked you before.

If you feel a little silly doing this, perhaps make it into a party game or do it over a few drinks. Life doesn't have to be so serious all the time – have fun!

59.

Spend 10 or 20 minutes getting creative in a new way. If you usually write, try drawing. If you're into painting, try journalling for a change. Perhaps pick up an instrument. Try dancing or singing or, I don't know, expressing yourself through mime. Just mix it up and see what happens.

Creativity helps us in all sorts of ways, but sometimes we get stuck in a rut doing the same creative thing whenever we want to take a break, relax, or express ourselves. Mixing it up can get our juices flowing, it can show us talents we perhaps didn't realise we had, and it can help us release all that stress we've been bottling up. Creativity – whatever kind it is – can be incredibly therapeutic.

60.

Consider the answers to the following questions: What does happiness mean to you? And how can you make yourself happy?

One of my mentors, Lori Harder, asks her guests this at the end of every podcast, and it's something we don't often think about. So, go on – what does happiness mean to you? And what can you do to make yourself happy?

There are no right or wrong answers here, so give it a good think and write down whatever you come up with. Then, ask yourself: If you know what you need to do to make yourself happy but you're not doing it, *why* aren't you doing it? And what can you do to overcome any obstacles standing in your way?

61.

Reframe your mindset around: rejection.

Rejection. We've all been there. Whether it's with relationships, jobs, new opportunities, friendships, school... whatever it is, it sucks. It makes us feel terrible. Sick to the stomach.

Therefore, we actively avoid rejection whenever we can – we go out of our way to make sure we don't even put ourselves in a position where we can be rejected. We don't ask out that person we want to ask out. We don't apply for that new job. We don't ask for that promotion or raise. We don't ask someone who could be a new friend out for a coffee. If we don't put ourselves out there, there's no chance of being rejected, right?

Right, but also wrong. This is no way to live. This whole book is all about getting out of your comfort zone and growing as a person, and none of that is possible if we're not willing to get rejected. Just like with failure, rejection is inevitable, so we need to learn not to take it so personally (easier said than done, I know).

So, what do we do? We think of it as a numbers game. Take famous authors who published their book after being rejected by 10, 20, or 30 publishers. Each rejection would have been like a punch in the gut, yet they kept going.

If your book is good and you keep approaching publishers, you'll probably get there, even if it takes years. If you approach bloggers online, asking them to feature your product or service or story, most of them will probably say no (at least at first). Eventually, though, one will say yes, and you'll be glad you kept trying.

It's a numbers game, and every 'no' is a no for a reason – it just means that person you're trying to get on side is not the right fit for you, right now. Happily collect your 'no', knowing it's not right for you, and carry on.

When we stop taking rejection so personally and instead just see it as a numbers game – see how many 'nos' you can collect! The more you collect, the sooner you'll get your yes! – rejection becomes a lot easier to take. And the more you put yourself out there and the more you get rejected, the less of a big deal it becomes. It's just part of the process. Accept the no and carry on to the next.

62.

Choose a song or a piece of music that really speaks to you and motivates you, whether it be motivational in terms of work, exercise, or simply getting up off your ass and getting on with things.

Then, make it your 'motivational song' and listen to it whenever you need to get to work and get shit done.

If you're not sure where to start with this one, try googling 'motivational songs' or 'uplifting music', or perhaps take a look at some ready-made playlists on apps such as Spotify, Amazon Music, or iTunes. You might even find whole new genres or artists you hadn't heard before.

63.

Think back to your favourite ever holiday. Spend some time reminiscing about where you went, what you did, and the best spots you visited.

If you have photos from this holiday, spend a while sorting through them and choosing some to print (either at home or using a printing service online). You can then create a nice little display of the photos and put them up somewhere in your house, reminding you of the best holiday you ever had and encouraging you to either go there again or go somewhere else that's equally amazing.

I did this with photos of a road trip I took with a couple of friends around New England in the autumn. I took nine photos off my Instagram account, so they were already filtered and edited and looking awesome, and printed them off. Then I arranged them on a nice background in three rows, looking like the Instagram photo grid.

They're in my room by my bed and I see them every day, reminding me of how awesome that trip was. I chose photos of places and landscapes over people and objects, so my particular grid of photos is filled with pumpkins, autumn leaves and trees, and some of the beautiful buildings we visited. Take me back there now!

64.

Write out a sentence describing yourself as the person you are now. Then write out another sentence describing the person you want to be/how you'd like to be described by others.

What are the differences? Is the person you want to be fitter? Healthier? Do you dress in a different way? Do you hold yourself differently? Are you more confident, more groomed, more stylish? Do you smile more? Laugh more? Get specific with the details.

Then write out a list of things you can do to start working towards being that second person, and keep them in mind as you work your way through the rest of the prompts.

If I were doing this, I'd no doubt be fitter and healthier than I am (as I'm always working on being a fitter, healthier version of myself), I'd probably be more stylish and wear better clothes, I'd perhaps have a different haircut that I haven't tried out yet, or different make-up, and I'd hold my head higher, projecting confidence and good, positive energy at all times.

65.

Major self-plugging moment here – why not give The Travel Transformation Podcast a listen? (Psst... it's my podcast.)

Even if you're not particularly into travel, I really think some of the topics I cover can help motivate, inspire, and encourage you to go after all your big goals.

Find out more at traveltransformationcoach.com/podcast.

66.

Find yourself a mentor. This can be a friend, someone in your family, even a colleague at work – as long as they know something you want to know, or do something you want to do, and as long as you trust them to help you.

If you can't find one in 'real life', look online, or choose a famous mentor who can teach you through their books, articles, podcasts, videos, and so on.

Joining online groups and clubs can be a great way of meeting mentors. Alternatively, think about someone already in your life who you admire and ask them if they'd like to grab a drink or a bite to eat in exchange for asking them some questions. You never know where it might lead!

67.

It's time to get some accountability, because putting some much-needed skin in the game can make all the difference.

So, I want you to tell everyone and anyone you can think of – in person and online – that you're making your way through this book, and describe any 'wins' you've had so far

– or anything you're struggling with. This will help you make connections with like-minded individuals, and perhaps you'll even find an accountability buddy to go through the rest of the book with.

I really do believe that your journey through this book will be greatly enhanced if you share your progress with others, whether it's your closest friends and family members or totally random strangers on the internet. They could really help, and they won't be strangers for long (she said, in an incredibly cheesy manner).

68.

Here's a basic prompt for you: Cut down on your alcohol intake.

Obviously, this only applies to people who drink alcohol, but if you do, consider drinking a little less – you don't have to go teetotal.

Alcohol can affect our bodies in so many ways, and I'm not just talking hangovers. We might feel hungrier and eat more unhealthy food, which in turn makes us feel lethargic, it can disrupt our sleep, making us incredibly tired the next day, and it can just make us feel… well, shit.

I'm not saying you shouldn't drink alcohol – I love a good glass of wine or a nice flavoured gin – but if you're currently at a point in your life where you need to get stuff done, alcohol can really hold you back.

69.

Take a deep breath and tell yourself the following: "I am lucky to be alive. I am lucky to be breathing. I am lucky to have all the things I own. I am lucky to have all the wonderful people I have in my life. I am lucky to be here on this planet at this particular moment in time. I am SO lucky."

All too often we focus on the things we don't have in our lives and forget about all the amazing things we do have. We ARE lucky to be alive, so just take a moment to remind yourself of this fact.

70.

Go through your closet/wardrobe and try on all your clothes (you might have to spread this out over several days depending on how many clothes you have and how much spare time you have).

Appreciate every item you own and really take a moment to think about how awesome it is that you have all these wonderful clothes. Enjoy the colours and textures and how each piece makes you feel – and any memories it might bring up.

Then get rid of anything that is too big, too small, doesn't fit right, or that you just don't like anymore. Our styles change as we grow older, and sometimes we just feel like trying something new.

You can make this into a fun activity – put on some of your favourite music while you're doing it, and maybe have a glass of wine if you partake. Then, once you've cleared out your closet, you'll have far more room for any new clothes you might buy in the future, perhaps even coming up with a completely new style (or at least trying a new garment or two that you've never even thought of trying before).

71.

Pick one thing you've done (or that happened to you) over the past 24 hours and celebrate it, no matter how small or silly that thing might be. For instance, you could celebrate:

• Doing a workout when you really didn't feel like it.

• Eating your five a day – yay health!

• Making that phone call or sending that text you've been putting off for ages.

• Standing up for yourself and your boundaries.

• Saying 'no' to something you didn't want to do even though you felt pressured to say yes.

• Receiving kind words or praise at work.

Life is short, and it's so important to celebrate even the little things. Go on, give it a try!

How you celebrate is up to you. Make yourself a nice cup of tea and sit down for 10 minutes with a few biscuits and no distractions, watch an episode of your favourite TV show with a mug of hot chocolate, have a glass of wine and a dance, read some of your favourite book, order something online… whatever makes you happy. Go on, celebrate!

72.

Is there something you've always wanted to do but have never done, either because you didn't have the guts, you couldn't justify the price, or you've simply never got around to it? Well, now is the time to do it!

Or at least book it. Or at least put a date in your calendar sometime in the near future so that you can save up for the activity or whatever it is and book it when you have the money. Just make a promise to yourself that you WILL do it. It doesn't matter how big or small the thing might be. Examples include:

- Going skydiving (or indoor skydiving)
- Taking a guitar lesson
- Riding a horse
- Visiting some tourist attraction or landmark
- Writing that book you've been thinking about for years
- Sending a message to someone you admire
- Booking that weekend away at a fancy resort
- Having a day out somewhere local

Whatever it is, either book it or put a solid date in your diary when you WILL book it.

Life is too short and tomorrow isn't promised, so if there's something you want to do, do it while you still can!

73.

Get your notebook and write out the following:

I am grateful for today.

Then, read it back to yourself – out loud – several times. There is no guarantee that we'll have tomorrow. Be grateful for today.

We often forget the little things we should be grateful for, and writing them down and saying them out loud can help us remember.

74.

Can you trace your current job, relationship, or situation back to one moment or one person?

I can trace my career back to a guy who was temping at one of my old jobs. He casually mentioned how you could now self-publish ebooks on Amazon (this was a while ago). And so I did.

That's how I started making money with my writing and that's also how I met another self-published writer online who had his own copywriting agency. I did some work for him and then started up my own editing/proofreading/ghostwriting business, which then led to the creation of the Write Your Life Method and all the self-development stuff.

Pinpoint the exact moment or person that set you on your path, write it down, and be grateful for them.

And, if it is a person, perhaps let them know what they did for you – they might have no idea.

75.

Have a 'hygge' moment.

If you don't know what it is, 'hygge' is a Danish and Norwegian word and concept relating to cosiness, wellness, and contentment. You can have a hygge house, a hygge feeling, a hygge moment, and so on.

Think of warm, chunky blankets, tea and hot chocolate, a roaring fire, candles, fairy lights, curling up with a book, listening to the rain tapping against the window, putting on relaxing music, stroking a pet… anything that creates a calm, comforting atmosphere that makes you feel cosy and content.

So, what can you do right now to give yourself a hygge moment? For me it means getting a cup of my favourite type of tea and some high quality chocolate, curling up under a chunky blanket, and reading a book, away from any screens, devices, or responsibilities! Even if it's just for 10 minutes, give it a try.

This works particularly well in the cold, dark, dreary winter months when the weather's rubbish and you don't want to venture outside (or if you've just ventured outside and now want to come into the warm, getting cosy and comfy after braving the elements). Hygge means different things to different people, so find your own hygge – whatever it might be – and have your own hygge moment.

76.

There's a quote by John Burroughs that goes 'leap and the net shall appear', and it's how many entrepreneurs live their lives, especially when it comes to business.

In fact, there's also a quote about how entrepreneurs jump and build their parachute on the way down. While I wouldn't recommend this for actual skydiving, it's a great thing to keep in mind as we live our lives.

Starting before you're ready, for some people, is the only way they're ever going to start. They make excuses and put things off because it's 'not the right time'. Well, it's never going to be the right time, so do it now. Jump and build your parachute on the way down.

What can you apply this quote to in your life right now?

If there's something you've been putting off because the timing isn't perfect, stop it. Do it right now. Take the first step today. Just jump (figuratively, of course). You can always build your parachute on the way down, and the best part is? You won't be the only one working on building that parachute. During your journey you'll come across endless numbers of people willing to help you out, so what are you waiting for? Stop with the excuses and start before you're ready!

77.

Do you watch soap operas? Or dramas? Do you notice how people's problems or issues often get cleared up or sorted out within a few episodes? Perhaps, sometimes, it will take a few weeks or months – and yes, some storylines go on for years – but generally, a character has a problem, they battle with it, and then it gets solved (often to never be mentioned again!).

Well, what if you did that in your own life? Think of a problem you currently have, perhaps one you've had for years and have never done anything about. Then imagine you're a character in a soap opera with that exact same problem.

The fact that you've done nothing about it for YEARS would be driving the audience mad by now. They'd be asking, 'Why hasn't she done anything about this?' or saying things like, 'That would drive me crazy, having a problem like that and never doing anything to solve it!'

So, with this in mind, what would your 'character' do about the problem? If it's a soap, they'd probably talk to someone else about it, right? Or they'd go to therapy, or they'd have a big discussion about it with their neighbours. One way or another, it would get solved. So, why not give it a go?

Yes, I know soap operas aren't real, and that in real life our problems and issues are often a lot more complex and take a lot more time to solve or get over, but just give it a chance. This is simply a fun exercise designed to help you look at your problems from another angle.

78.

Spare a thought for your ancestors. That's right – I want you to think of the people who came before you, in particular those you're related to, and perhaps go back 100 years, 200 years, or 300 years.

Even if you've never even attempted a family tree or know nothing about your ancestors, I think we can all imagine how they might have lived their lives and how different those lives would have been compared to our lives today.

For instance, I'm pretty sure my ancestors living 200 years ago wouldn't have anywhere near as many advantages as I do today (the women in particular).

So, take out your notebook and make a list of all the things you have now that they would be baffled and amazed by (your phone, your laptop, your house, your car, your career), and then write down all the things you think your ancestors would think about you. Would they be happy for you? Proud of what you've achieved? Amazed by what humans in general have achieved?

Then think about your future family, the people who will come after you. What things will they achieve? And will their achievements be based on what you're working on now and on how you're growing and developing as a person right now? I wouldn't be able to vote now if it weren't for the Suffragettes, for instance. So, how are you going to help out future generations?

Looking at our lives in this way – and reminding ourselves that we're just one individual in a long line of individuals – can help us to see ourselves in a completely different way. Be grateful for what the people who have come before you have done, and think about what you can do for the people who will come after you.

79.

We all know the phrase 'a problem shared is a problem halved', and while this isn't true in every instance, I do think it's a good rule of thumb in general.

We often keep our issues to ourselves, thinking it's some huge thing we could never tell anyone else, but when we finally do tell someone else, we don't know what we were so worried about.

Either it doesn't seem like such a huge deal once you've said it out loud, or the person you've told will be able to help you with your issue, offering advice and suggestions – or just being there for moral support.

Have a think: have you been holding onto something or bottling it up for fear of what other people might think? And do you have someone in your life who you could talk to about it?

Even just coming up with the name of the person you could talk to, if you decide to, can feel like a huge weight has been lifted. And who knows? Maybe in the next few days you'll find the courage to actually tell them.

We all know that bottling up emotions and fears is bad for us, and yet we do it all the time. Even if the person you tell has no practical advice or suggestions on how to solve your problem, just saying the words out loud (or typing them in a message) can really help and can change how you feel about the problem or issue. Give it a go – it could change your life.

80.

Here's a fun one. Spend a few minutes thinking about/searching for a song or piece of music that you think either embodies you as a person or embodies the person you want to be (preferably as epic a piece of music as you can find). Think of it as your very own personal 'soundtrack' song, and download it to your phone or whatever you listen to music on.

Then start playing it at certain points of the day – when you're getting up, when you're in the shower, when you're getting dressed, and so on. Use it to either psyche yourself up or calm yourself down (depending on the song). Use it regularly. This is the soundtrack to your very own personal movie.

This is another one you might think is a little silly, but try it anyway. If you're not sure where to start with picking out music, take a look at some playlists on Spotify or Apple Music – search for 'epic movie soundtracks' or something like that. You might find some new music you're into as well – bonus.

81.

If you have an issue or problem that you don't know how to solve (or a decision you don't know how to make), take a step 'outside' of yourself and look at the situation from the outside in.

Imagine you were talking to a close friend and they were describing the problem or the decision they needed to make.

What would you tell them? What advice would you give them? Would you comfort them? Give them words of encouragement? Any practical instructions or guidance? Would you go easy on them or be harsh to them, telling them to 'man up' or stop being so whiny? (I'd hope you wouldn't, but the point here is that if you wouldn't say those things to a friend, make sure you're not saying them to yourself).

Write down what you'd say, then read it back, out loud: you've just given yourself some (hopefully useful) advice.

Many of us find it so easy to give advice to other people, or to comfort our friends when they're feeling down or confused about something. Many of us find it difficult to extend the same courtesy to ourselves, or to see our own circumstances from a different point of view. This exercise, therefore, can be really helpful.

82.

Warning: this one's a morbid one!

Imagine you're at the end of your life, on your deathbed (or whatever that might look like) on your last day on earth.

Imagine that, in your last breaths, your life flashes in front of your eyes – but a slow flash, so you can see each and every prominent memory. Now imagine that day is today. Right now. This very moment.

If your life flashed in front of your eyes right now, what would those memories tell you? Would they be mostly good ones, or mostly bad ones? Would you regret any of them? Would you regret the memories you never got to make and, if so, which things in particular would you wish you'd done? How would you feel when watching these memories? Proud? Guilty? Happy? Sad? Positive? Negative? Write down how you'd be feeling.

Then, if it's a bad emotion, write down what you would need to do right now to change that emotion, so that when it does come to your last day on earth, you watch those memories back feeling nothing but happiness, love, satisfaction, and peace, knowing you did everything you could to help your loved ones, and knowing you achieved everything you set out to achieve (and more).

You can also write down some ideas of memories you hope to see, especially if you haven't experienced them yet. For instance, I'd like to see less time spent indoors, in the same house, and more time travelling!

This is a morbid prompt, as I said, but it's also a really important one. None of us know how long we have left on this planet, and the vast majority of us will not know when we wake up one day that it's going to be our last. Terrifying. Also, highly motivational.

83.

If you don't have any (or many), go and buy yourself a plant (or a few) – and preferably one off NASA's list of air-purifying house plants (yes, such a list exists).

Not only do these plants brighten up the place and look all nice and green, they also remove nasty toxins from the air and reduce symptoms such as headaches and eye irritations.

If you work from home and it's too cold to have the windows open all the time to let some fresh air in, these plants are a great alternative. Plus, if you live on your own or get lonely during your work from home workday, you've now got someone (erm, I mean… something…) to talk to. Bonus!

Personally, I have a peace lily and a mother-in-law's tongue/snake plant to help when I'm working from home (which is all the time), plus a yucca called Eugene because… well… why not?

84.

'Get better sleep' prompt: Come up with a wind-down routine and stick to it.

Start winding down half an hour or an hour before bed, and try to do the same thing every day. This could include things like taking a bath, doing some meditation, writing in a journal, doing a gratitude practice, reading, and then listening to a sleep app or podcast as you drift off.

Do the same thing every night, as this will signal to your brain that it's time to start getting sleepy. Remember: sleep is so incredibly important, so anything you can do to minimise distractions and help you get a better night's sleep is well worth doing.

85.

Find your pet and give them a big hug (depending on what pet you have – if it's a fish, for example, I wouldn't recommend doing this).

Spend some time just sitting with them, stroking them, and talking to them, without any other distractions. Studies suggest that doing this helps to relax us, and can even help lower blood pressure, so it's extremely good for you.

If you don't have a pet, do you know anyone who does? Go and visit a family member or friend who has one (but don't tell them you're only visiting to make use of their cat/dog/whatever they have), or maybe volunteer at an animal shelter for an afternoon.

Obviously, if you have a pet, I recommend doing this every day and as much as possible, because animals are awesome – but this is more about taking the time to be present with your pet without any distractions, and really taking a few moments for yourself, with the bonus of an amazing furry (or otherwise) friend by your side.

86.

Get out your notebook and write down your top five fictional characters (or just five characters you admire). These can be from books, from films, from TV shows… wherever.

Then write down five qualities for each character that describes who they are as a person – use just one word per quality, such as 'resilient', 'strong', 'kind', 'generous', 'brave', 'cheerful', 'positive', 'thoughtful', and so on.

You should now have 25 qualities – five for each character. Circle any qualities that have been repeated, either with the exact same word or words that mean similar things. What are the main words you've circled?

Now, write out the five main qualities you'd use to describe yourself. Do any of them match? If none of them match, how can you make your qualities more like the qualities you admire in the fictional characters?

Personally, I tend to gravitate towards strong female characters, like Buffy Summers in *Buffy the Vampire Slayer*, Arya Stark in *Game of Thrones*, and Wynonna Earp from, well, *Wynonna Earp*. They're all strong, resilient, brave warrior women who fight for their families and for what they believe in. I'm definitely not a warrior woman, so I've got some work to do!

87.

Organise your email inbox – and no, I'm not joking.

Whether it's your work inbox, your personal inbox, or a bit of both, we can often get overwhelmed by all the emails and messages we know are waiting for us.

I use Gmail, so I can access it anywhere, and I also have it linked to my phone – both a blessing and a curse. But it's fine, because I'm organised. I have several folders (admin, accounting, house stuff, random, editing business, write your life method, expenses, holidays, and so on), and every time an email comes in I either delete it straight away if I don't need it, file it away into a folder after I've read it/replied if needed, or keep it in my inbox until I've dealt with it – usually within a day or so. I don't let my inbox get clogged up, so I'm not overwhelmed by emails. When you work online, that's a big deal.

This is one of those prompts that might sound ridiculous to you, and you might not need to do it, but I love organising, and I love decluttering, and this is just a digital version of that. I also check my spam every day in case something important has found its way in there (as it sometimes does), and also get rid of the 'trash'. Ah, lovely clean inbox. What a great feeling.

88.

Do an 'accountability buddy' test. Sometimes, we need to be held accountable for the things we say we're going to do, so telling others we're going to do it can help. But is your accountability buddy really going to make you stick to your word? Why not test it out?

For instance, think of something easy you know you can do and tell your accountability buddy you're going to complete that task in the next five days. Make it clear that you need them to hold you accountable to it. Then wait.

If you accountability buddy sends you a message on day five and says, "Hey! Did you do the thing? Show me proof!" then you know you've got a good one. If they don't contact you on day five, or six, or seven, and if they never mention the thing again, it's probably time to find a different accountability buddy.

This isn't lying – you should actually complete the thing, so that when your accountability buddy does ask you if you've done it, you can hold your head high and say, "Yes! I did the thing! Thank you, accountability buddy, for keeping me on track." Then ask them to keep you accountable for something you can't do quite as easily.

89.

Think of something you're (currently) scared about. Applying for that new job? Taking a driving test? Asking someone on a date? Starting a side hustle? Jumping out of a plane?

Whatever it is, I want you to consider: are you actually scared of it, or is it just excitement in a fancy hat?

Take a moment and really ponder if you're scared about this new thing (and everything it represents) or if you're excited about what this new thing might lead to. Write it down.

If you *are* scared of something, ask yourself why you're scared, and write down the answer. Keep asking yourself 'why' or 'why does that matter' until you get to the root cause, the core issue.

For instance, 'I'm scared of starting my new business.' Why? 'Because I don't know what I'm doing.' Why does that matter? 'Because I don't want to look like a fraud.' Why does that matter? 'Because I don't want people judging me.' Why? 'Because I care what people think and I don't want them to reject me.' So, your fear of starting a new business is actually a fear of potential rejection. Give it a go.

This also works for other issues you're having. Just keep asking yourself 'why' and 'why does that matter' and keep drilling down until you get to the core of the issue.

90.

Another organisational prompt! If you have your own business (or are starting one), or have several projects/hobbies on the go, or just have a lot going on in your life right now, I recommend using a program like Trello to keep track of everything.

You can get it for free, and it's a really easy way of breaking down projects into tasks. It works really well if you share the Trello board with someone else too – a partner, a work colleague, an assistant, and so on. Keep track of everything and don't let yourself get overwhelmed with all the balls you're trying to keep up in the air.

I have several Trello boards for several things. I have one for my proofreading and editing business, one for my Write Your Life work, one for my other projects, and one shared with my virtual assistant to keep track of content for my website and social media. You can also make them pretty with different colours and backgrounds which, of course, is the main thing.

91.

Buy yourself some flowers to brighten up your desk, or your bedroom or kitchen. You don't have to wait for someone else to buy them for you!

It's amazing how even something as simple as a little bouquet of flowers can brighten your day, especially if you go for your favourite flowers or your favourite colours. Make sure you put them where you'll see them – and be able to smell them – throughout the day.

92.

Take some photos! Grab your smartphone and just start taking photos around your house, garden, or while out on a walk.

I love getting creative with taking pictures, and I particularly love editing them on Instagram and trying out different filters before posting them online.

Photography can teach us so many things about looking at things from different angles, taking a mundane object and making it interesting, and capturing the beauty in everyday life. And, these days, you don't even need a fancy camera to do it.

My phone is FULL of photos. I take so many of them, whether for content for work or for 'personal use', and I love playing around with filters and various editing apps and programs. If you don't have Instagram try using Snapseed or Prisma Photo Editor.

93.

Get a cup of herbal tea (this might involve going out and buying some if you don't have any – personally, I am extremely British in that I have a whole 'tea station' going on in my kitchen) and sit down for five minutes to really enjoy it.

Make it something soothing, like chamomile, or refreshing, like peppermint. You could even get some of those flowering teas and watch the little flower unfold in your teapot or cup. I love those. Breathe in the scent, hold your mug in your hands to warm you up (if you're somewhere cold, anyway!) and just clear your mind for the number of minutes it takes you to finish the tea. Aahhh, that's better.

I love all kinds of tea, but here are some of my favourites: Yorkshire Gold, jasmine tea, peppermint tea, anything made by Pukka but in particular their peppermint and liquorice, any type of chai, chamomile, and anything by Celestial Seasonings, though my favourites are Sweet Harvest Pumpkin, Bengal Spice, Tension Tamer, Fast Lane, Candy Cane Lane, Sugar Cookie Sleigh Ride, and – of course – Sleepytime. Excuse me while I go and put the kettle on…

94.

Find or buy a nice notebook and make it into your 'Nice Words Notebook'.

Stay with me here. This is basically a book where you write down anything positive anyone says to you, whether it's someone giving you a compliment, praising your work, encouraging you to go after something, giving you/your company a review or testimonial, or just saying something nice to you that brightens your day.

Write down the words whenever you come across one of these situations, and do it before you forget. Then, if you ever have a day when you're feeling down about yourself/your work/your life, you can take out the book and read through it, reminding yourself just how awesome you are – and just how many people you have rooting for you.

This might seem a little weird, but I have my very own Nice Words Notebook and I use it all the time. I haven't re-read it in a while, but even just the act of writing out, by hand (in a nice pen, of course), all the great feedback you get from other people can make you feel awesome. I use it mainly for reviews, testimonials, and nice emails I get from clients and people who have read my books, or from friends who send encouraging messages about my business. It definitely helps to keep your spirits up!

95.

Can you think of a time when you were in pain, or when something had gone wrong, or when the entire world seemed to be falling down around you, and where – ultimately – something good came out of it? A new job? A new house? A new relationship? A new direction in life? A new way of looking at things? A new appreciation for something or someone?

Write down the thing that happened to you – or the situation you found yourself in – and then write a list of all the good things that came out of it. I'm sure, if you really spent some time thinking about it, you could come up with lots of examples.

Then, when bad things happen in the future, you can look back at this list and remind yourself that no matter what happened, good things *can* come out of bad times.

Changing our mindset around the pain we experience can change the way we look at everything.

96.

If you don't use a daily calendar to organise your tasks, consider getting one.

I honestly don't know where I'd be without my Google Calendar – probably flailing around all day, wondering what on earth I'm meant to be doing next.

I like to-do lists, sure, but something about structuring your day in a calendar, with certain times for certain tasks (and, of course, colour-coded blocks) really helps me see what I have to achieve that day, and exactly when I'm going to get each little task done.

In fact, I use Google Calendar, Trello, Excel spreadsheets, and the Google Keep app on my phone to keep track of all my tasks. A little overkill, perhaps, but it works for me.

97.

Reframe your mindset around: past relationships.

The 'past' in 'past relationships' suggests that those relationships didn't work out, whether they were romantic ones, friendships, or anything else. This implies something went wrong with them, therefore these types of relationships can be difficult to look back on. It's painful to relive these relationships, and to think about the people who are no longer in our lives.

So, it's time to reframe how we think about them. Even if a relationship ended badly, I'm sure there's something you can take from it – something you can learn, something you may have already used in a different relationship going forward, some knowledge you've gained from the experience. If you think really hard, you might come up with lots of things you can take from it.

If you can't think of any knowledge gained or lessons learnt from a particular relationship, I'm sure there's still something good that happened when you were in the relationship, even if it was something small. You might have had a great time on a holiday or day out with that person, you might have met a really good friend through that person, or perhaps they introduced you to a band you like or one of your favourite TV shows or movies. Write down everything you can think of, and reframe how you think about that person and that relationship.

Even the truly sucky relationships can give us something good, even if that something good is us growing as a result of going through a terrible time, or us coming out of a horrible relationship as a stronger person. You don't have to like the person to have gained something from them, whether directly or indirectly.

98.

Choose one thing you'd like to achieve over the next 30 days and commit to doing it.

What's something you've been putting off? Or something you don't think you will physically be able to do? Well, it's time to do it – whether you believe in yourself or not. Your actions will tell you otherwise; when you achieve the thing, you'll believe you can do whatever you set your mind to.

A prompt a day is great, but sometimes we need to look a little more into the future – and give ourselves a little more time – to achieve our goals.

99.

Go on Instagram, Facebook, Twitter, LinkedIn, or whatever your preferred social media platform is, and comment on someone's post saying something positive, complimentary, encouraging, or just plain nice.

This can be a friend, family member, colleague, or a complete stranger, it doesn't matter. Your words will give them a boost, and it will give you a boost too.

And you don't have to stop at just one. Why not give out five compliments, or 10 nice messages? Just make sure you mean what you say and that you're sincere in your praise. And don't go overboard if it's someone you don't know – a lot of people find it hard to accept compliments, and therefore might get freaked out.

100.

Do some doodling.

For some reason, doodling always calms me down, and I often find myself doodling (mindlessly, without really realising I'm doing it) while on a long phone call or when waiting for someone to ring me.

Just put on some music, get a nice-coloured pen, and do some 'free doodling'. Hopefully, it will free up your mind and help you relax.

Often, ideas come to me when I'm doodling. As one part of my brain is focused on the – extremely easy – task of making pretty swirls and shapes on the paper, another part of my brain can be figuring something out, something that's been bothering me recently or a problem I've yet to find a solution for. It can work almost as well as getting up and getting your body moving, which can also allow your brain to come up with some epic ideas.

101.

Continuing on from the Nice Words Notebook prompt, consider typing up some of these compliments/messages, then printing them out (in different fonts and colours, if you so desire) and putting them up on a board or in a frame where you'll see it regularly.

I've done this with reviews of my *Write Your Life* book. I have one pin board next to my desk which is my vision board, filled with photos and quotes, and then another pin board right next to it which is my review board. Then, whenever I'm feeling overwhelmed with work or feeling like I'm not getting anywhere, all I need to do is glance over at my two boards and, suddenly, I'm filled with motivation again!

If you don't want to do a pin board, just put your Nice Words Notebook somewhere you'll see it on a regular basis, so you don't forget it (or all the nice words it's filled with). Or you could put some of your favourite Nice Words quotes together as an image to use as your computer desktop.

102.

If you drive and have a car, go for a spin by yourself, with no particular destination in mind, and see where you end up (it might be somewhere awesome, or somewhere you've never been before, or at the house of a friend you haven't seen in years).

But, the main thing I want you to do on this journey is to put on some of your favourite music and sing along at the top of your lungs (while still focusing on the road, of course).

This can be so freeing, especially if your home situation means you don't get to do this in your house. If you don't drive/have a car, ask a trusted friend if they want to go for a drive with you (but warn them about the singing, otherwise it might come as a bit of a shock).

I love doing this. There's no chance of the neighbours hearing you, and even if a pedestrian or someone does hear you as you drive past, it doesn't matter because you'll soon be zooming away, out of their vicinity (unless you're stuck in a traffic jam, I suppose). It also gives you the chance to listen to whatever you want, without your partner or children or whoever scrabbling to put on their favourite music. Enjoy the 'me' time.

103.

'Get better sleep' prompt: Try using earplugs to stop any noise distractions.

Earplugs are great if you have noisy neighbours, a snoring partner, teenagers staying up late, or any other noises that might stop you from falling asleep easily. These days, you can get all different kinds of earplugs too. Remember: sleep is so incredibly important, so anything you can do to minimise distractions and help you get a better night's sleep is well worth doing.

104.

Take a walk and smile at five or more people – making eye contact and everything.

This might not seem like such a huge deal to some of you, but in some places it's not really the norm to make eye contact with everyone you pass by on the street or in the supermarket, let alone – gasp! – actually smile at them.

In some parts of the UK, if you do this, people might actually think you're some kind of psychopath – no joke. So, unless you live in a place where this kind of behaviour could result in a hostile reaction, give it a try.

It really is amazing what something as simple as a smile can do for your mood and the mood of the person on the receiving end. You never know; they could be having the worst day ever, and a smile from a stranger could turn their whole perception of their day around. Also, smiling makes you feel good. It just does.

105.

Go out and start a conversation with a stranger. Again, to some people this might not be a big deal at all, but to some people – introverts, for instance, or people with social anxiety – it can be really difficult to put themselves out there.

It doesn't have to be anything major, either. Mention something to the person in the queue at the shop about the weather (hey, I'm British, it's what we do) or about the time of year, or about anything at all. The person might reply and continue the conversation or not, it doesn't matter – just opening your mouth and making the first move is the goal here.

You never know where this could go. You might, for instance, be stuck in a queue for ages, and talking to the person next to you might make the time seem to go by faster. You might have a good time, laughing with the other person, and it might even be the start of a beautiful friendship. Or you might be counting down the seconds until you can escape the person and get the hell out of there... it could go either way. But just give it a try and see!

106.

Give a compliment (one you really mean) to a complete stranger.

I find this easier to do in certain situations. For instance, if you're a woman in a nightclub, having a few drinks, and then you go to the ladies' room, this is incredibly easy to do. "Oh my god, I love your shoes! Ooh, where did you get your lipstick from? It's gorgeous. How do you get your hair to stay like that all night?" and so on. It might be rather stereotypical, but it's true.

In other situations, it might be a bit trickier. If you feel uncomfortable doing this, pose it as a question rather than a standalone compliment. For instance, if you see someone walking past in epic boots, instead of just shouting, "Hey! Cool boots!" you can go up to the person and say, "Hi, I just wanted to know where you got your boots from? They're amazing and I'd love to get myself a pair!" Voila. Compliment given (and hopefully some useful boot intel received as well).

I'm sure you've been on the end of random compliments before – ones you weren't expecting – and it makes you feel good, doesn't it? Even if you're British (or with British tendencies) and averse to receiving compliments like I sometimes am, after we get past the awkwardness and the confusion of what to say in return, it still gives us a warm glow to be told something like that.

107.

Have an impromptu photo shoot. You can do this on your own, with your partner, with your kids, with your friends, or whoever, and you can do it in the house, in your garden, or out and about, like on a walk or in a bar.

Wear different outfits, try different make-up or hairstyles, use props, use filters... put some music on while you're doing it, grab a drink or have some snacks, and have fun.

Sometimes we just need to revert to childhood and indulge in play. And, with modern smartphones, filters, and apps to post them on, photo shoots are more fun than ever.

If you don't like taking photos of yourself (and if you don't, you should try anyway, because I'm sure you're awesome!) then have a photo shoot where your family members or friends are the subjects of the pictures, or perhaps a pet, or anything else you want to take photos of. Photograph your plants or your flowers or your beauty products... it's up to you! Just make sure it's light-hearted and fun.

108.

If you have Instagram, try shooting a Reel. These are funny or educational short videos that you can add filters, text, and music to, and they're used by businesses, brands, and people with personal profiles.

They're really fun to create, and a little addictive too – so be warned! In fact, even if you don't have Instagram, you could sign up and start creating Reels. Check out Reels made by other people to get you started.

Reels are great fun, and they're even more fun if you make them with friends, so get some friends over and give it a go!

109.

Write a letter to yourself from your future self – your future self that has achieved all your wildest dreams.

What would you say to yourself now if you knew that you were going to absolutely smash every single one of your goals and, ultimately, create your dream life?

Write down all the words of encouragement, comfort, and support you'd give your past self. Then read it through again. These are the words you need to be saying to yourself on a regular basis in order to smash all your goals and create your dream life.

I love this exercise. You can also imagine that your future self visits you, telling you that you're successful in the future and that you've achieved everything you're working so hard to achieve. Would that make you stop working now, make you give up striving so hard because you know you're going to be successful? No, it would make you work harder and it would make your desire for that dream life so much stronger. A self-fulfilling prophecy. It's fun to think about, anyway.

110.

Grab a pen and notepad and write down 10-20 things you really like about yourself.

We often get so bogged down in the negatives and what we don't like about ourselves that it can be easy to forget the things we do like. These can be about our personality, our physical appearance, our skills and talents, and so on – whatever you can think of. So, I might write:

- I like my kind, generous nature.
- I like how I'm a huge animal lover.
- I like how I donate to charity regularly.
- I think I'm a good friend.
- I like that I'm good at proofreading and spotting mistakes.
- I like the colour of my eyes.
- I like my creative side.
- I like how I'm constantly trying new things.
- I like how I never give up, even when it's hard.
- I like my long eyelashes.
- I like how I love learning.

This is a great exercise to do every time you're feeling down about yourself, or if something happens that makes you feel bad. If you want to, you can also ask someone else to do this exercise with you, but with them writing down things they like about you and vice versa. Do this with a partner or a good friend, or perhaps a close family member. It's also a good bonding activity to do with someone you're not as close to as you'd like to be.

111.

'Get better sleep' prompt: Use an aromatherapy roller ball on certain pulse points on your face, such as your temples.

These are great – I have one called 'Sweet Dreams' made by Tisserand. Remember: sleep is so incredibly important, so anything you can do to minimise distractions and help you get a better night's sleep is well worth doing.

112.

If you had to create a logo for yourself (like you'd do if you were starting a business), what would it be? Have a go at designing it!

Mine would most definitely be purple (my favourite colour – a rich, deep, Cadbury-type purple) and it would probably have a retro vibe to it. It would include an animal of some sort (probably a dog) as I love animals, and maybe a book or pen to illustrate my work and my creativity. And it would probably all be encompassed in a map of the world, showing off my love of travelling. I'd use big bold fonts, possibly in white to show up on the purple, and it would be eye-catching and striking to look at (how I want my life to be).

Go on, take a few minutes to design your own!

This exercise is just for fun, but if you really wanted to, you could go one step further and draw it out properly/create it on the computer/get someone else to create it for you. You could pop it on your vision board or on your desk, or put it as your phone background.

113.

Put together a 'harvest box' or care package for someone you know, or for someone you don't know very well in your community who could do with some help.

I used to love making harvest boxes when I was at primary school; everyone in the school would make one, filling it with fruit and vegetables and other types of food, and then they'd give them out to the elderly people in our village.

Make one for a relative or friend, or ask in a local Facebook or meet-up group if anyone knows of anyone who could benefit from one, then go and deliver it to them.

This is also a great exercise to do with other people. Get the whole family involved or gather some of your friends together. You can do the shopping together, and then spend some time together as you make up the boxes, preferably putting them in some nice little baskets and making them look visually appealing as well as appealing to the stomach. This can be a great thing to do at a certain time every year (say, harvest time, or at Christmas, and so on).

114.

Switching Perspectives Exercise. Write down the biggest problem you're having in your life right now that concerns another person. For instance, perhaps someone you were dating ghosted you. Perhaps you're having constant arguments with your partner. Maybe you haven't talked to a family member in years due to some ancient grudge. Or perhaps you're angry at someone for something they said.

Now, write out a sentence or two explaining the situation and then turn it around – do the old switcheroo (that's the technical term). Rewrite those couple of sentences as if you were the 'other person' in the scenario. As if you were the one ghosting someone, you were the one starting arguments or picking fights, you were the one who had said the hurtful thing.

Then write out a list of all the potential reasons that person might have for doing what they did, but write it in the first person as if *you* were that person – and only write out the explanations you think are believable, reasonable, and forgivable. For instance, having constant arguments with your partner. What could explain this behaviour? (And remember to write it in first person):

1. I'm not sleeping well, therefore I have no energy, therefore I'm not eating well, therefore I'm feeling groggy and lethargic, and I'm taking it out on other people. It has nothing to do with them and everything to do with how I'm feeling.

2. I feel like whenever we talk, we don't listen to what the other person is actually trying to say; we're just waiting for our turn to speak, which is really frustrating. Perhaps we need to figure out a different way of talking to each other.

3. We're arguing more because we're spending more time together than ever before – there's bound to be an adjustment period.

There. You've just made the villain of the situation into the hero of the piece. Or, if not the hero, at least someone whose perspective you now understand a little better. Perhaps that person isn't the baddie after all? Perhaps there is no baddie here? Does that help give you an idea of what to do about this situation now?

As part of this exercise, you could even ask the other person to create their own list, or to look at yours and see if any of these reasons are true, or at least let them know that you've been thinking about the situation from their point of view. Sometimes, even just admitting this can be enough to get you talking again, and – hopefully – resolving the issue or issues that brought you to this point.

115.

Some studies have come to the conclusion that we have over 6,000 thoughts each day, and many of those are the same, day in, day out (and I'm assuming, for many of us, a lot of those thoughts won't be positive ones).

Well, it's time to reprogram your brain with some new, positive thoughts. Throughout the day, I want you to think the following thoughts (and the more you think them, the better!):

• I am awesome.

• I am exactly where I need to be in life, right now.

- I can do anything I set my mind to.

- I have wonderful friends and family.

- I am bursting with potential and have so many opportunities ahead of me.

- I have a bright, exciting future.

- I rock.

As I've said before, self-talk is so important, and the kinder we are to ourselves in our thoughts, the more positive we'll feel in general.

116.

Try some free writing. Give yourself a topic (either vague or specific, such as 'my job' or 'what I really want to be doing') and just start writing.

Don't think too much or worry about spelling, grammar, or sentence structure – just write. You might be surprised at what you come up with, such as any insights you might have into a certain subject that you weren't even aware of, or some ideas of how to solve a problem or issue you're having. Give it a whirl.

When you're done, read it back and see if you've come up with any words of wisdom, or see if anything stands out to you as something you need to spend more time and/or effort on in your life.

This can be done with pen and paper or on a computer (if you're fast at typing – if not, it might stop you from writing as quickly as you're thinking). Just write whatever comes to mind, and don't worry about it making sense – you don't have to show it to anyone. You can keep this just for you.

117.

What did you enjoy doing when you were a child? Write out a list of anything and everything you can remember that made you smile, laugh, or just feel alive. For instance:

- I loved chocolate. In particular, I loved a good Freddo (back when they were super cheap).
- I loved being creative and messy, such as drawing or painting.
- I loved exploring the fields around my house with my best friend.
- I loved experimenting with make-up and hair products (hair mascara, anyone?), and I loved pretty much anything with glitter in it.
- I loved putting on some cheesy pop music and dancing around my bedroom.

Once you have your list, pick one thing off it (or all the things, if they're appropriate/applicable these days) and do it/eat it/drink it/whatever it is.

Do it today. Feel young again – even if just for a moment – and remind yourself of how easy it can be to get that rush of adrenaline, endorphins, and/or nostalgia.

If only Freddos hadn't gone up in price so dramatically!

118.

Parallel Universe Exercise. This could also be called the Sliding Doors Exercise, though I haven't seen that film in a long time so I'm not too sure it makes sense here.

Anyway, think of one huge decision you've made in your life. This could be deciding to go to university (or not), deciding which specific university or college to go to, getting married, moving towns or cities, making a career change, accepting a promotion, breaking up with someone, and so on.

First, write down the decision you made at the time. For instance, 'I decided to enrol in the American Studies programme at the University of Sussex' (which I did). Then think what would happen if you hadn't made this particular decision, and write down all the consequences of that action. For instance, in my example:

• I wouldn't have lived in Brighton for three years and met everyone I did at the University of Sussex.

• I wouldn't have had my year abroad in America – the best year of my life – and I wouldn't have met my friends at CU Boulder.

• I wouldn't have travelled around America for a month after the college semester ended, or gone on the several other trips I took throughout the year.

• I would have graduated university a whole year earlier without my year abroad, probably getting a different job and heading off in a completely different direction in life.

• I wouldn't have some of the best friends I have today, as I never would have met them.

- I wouldn't have gone on all the amazing holidays and trips I've been on with my uni friends over the years.

- I might have ended up living in a completely different part of the country, depending on where I'd decided to go to uni.

- If I'd decided not to go to university at all, I wouldn't have learnt so much over those four years (not just academically), and I wouldn't have had as much fun or had as many incredible experiences.

That one decision changed the course of my entire life, and guess what? That's true of any time in your life. If you're not where you want to be, or if you want more out of life, you're just one decision away from setting yourself on a completely different path. One decision away from heading out in a parallel universe and redesigning your entire life. And most decisions can be made in just a few seconds. That's kind of amazing, isn't it?

119.

Change something in your house that you've always wanted to change but have never quite got around to changing.

For instance, those curtains you've been putting up with because it seems like a hassle to pick out new ones, or replacing that old piece of kitchen equipment that doesn't work too well anymore.

Just change one thing, and it doesn't have to be anything expensive if you don't want to spend a lot of money. Use some paint you already have and give a piece of furniture a makeover, or throw something out (that one's free!) if you don't use it anymore.

We all spend a lot of time in our homes, so if there's something you don't like, change it! I'm currently eyeing up the curtains in my room and thinking there's got to be a better colour I could put up there. Off to the internet!

120.

Here's a basic prompt for you: Drink more water!

We all know we're supposed to drink eight glasses a day, or whatever the guidelines are for your country, but how many of us actually do it? I drink a lot of water, but I often have days where I know I don't drink enough, and my body lets me know: I get headaches and feel far less energetic than usual.

If you want to make water more interesting, cut some fruit up and pop it in your glass, or use a fruit infuser water bottle. You don't have to down it all at once, either; keep a large water bottle next to your desk, and take a few sips from it every half an hour – or whatever works for you. Keeping hydrated is so important and so easy to do, and it's amazing how many of us are constantly – and chronically – dehydrated.

121.

Go and carry out a random act of kindness. Let someone move ahead of you in the queue at the shop, let other drivers merge into traffic ahead of you, give up your seat on the bus or the train, pick up some litter and put it in the bin... just do something, no matter how small or insignificant it might seem. It all adds up.

This is another one we can introduce to our daily or weekly lives, so why not give it a go?

122.

Leave a treat or a nice note outside your door for your postman/delivery person. A snack, a drink, or just a heartfelt note thanking them for everything they do can really give them a boost as they go about their deliveries.

Many people do this at Christmas as a token of their appreciation, but why not surprise them by doing it at other times of the year? You could leave them an Easter egg at Easter, a cool drink on a hot summer's day, perhaps even some chocolates on Valentine's Day (just be aware that they might get the wrong end of the stick – unless, of course, you're actually trying to 'woo' your delivery person, in which case, go for it!).

123.

Get your notebook and write out the following:

I am grateful for the sky.

Read it back to yourself – out loud – several times and then look out the window or go outside and spend a moment just staring at the sky. Whether it's a bright blue sky with fluffy clouds, a black night sky with twinkling stars, or anything in between, I think you can agree it's pretty amazing.

We often forget the little things we should be grateful for, and writing them down and saying them out loud can help us remember.

124.

Buy a bouquet of flowers for someone to brighten their day.

It doesn't have to be a super expensive bouquet, and I'd recommend thinking outside the box with who you buy them for. Don't just get them for your partner – get them for your best friend, your parents, your kids, your grandparents, a work colleague who helped you out… anyone.

If you don't live near the person you want to buy flowers for, don't worry – that's what the internet's for. These days you can even get flowers that fit through people's letter boxes, so there's really no excuse for not getting that delivery sorted.

125.

'Pay it forward'.

For instance, if you're in a coffee shop and you're paying for your drink/food, offer to pay for the person next in line as well. Leave a bigger tip than usual (or at all, if you're in a country where tipping isn't the norm). Pay for someone's groceries if you have a full trolley and they're only waiting in line for one or two small items. Just little things like that.

This can seem like a bit of a weird thing to do at first, but the more you do it, the easier it becomes, and it really can brighten someone's day immeasurably (as well as your own). Then, hopefully, they'll go and pay it forward to someone else.

126.

Take an art class.

There are so many different types out there – drawing, painting, pottery, life drawing – so pick one, go with a friend, and have some fun.

You could even go to one of those 'art and wine' classes, where you get to drink wine with friends while being creative!

Take a look online and see if you can book one today.

Getting your creative juices flowing at home is all well and good, but trying it in a different setting – like in an art class, with other students and a teacher to help you, can make a nice change.

127.

Today, say no to something you don't usually say no to (within reason).

This is a bit vague, but apply it to whichever situation fits you best. For instance, if someone is taking advantage of your kindness and is constantly asking for favours, say no (nicely but firmly). Or if someone asks you to do something or go somewhere you really don't want to do/go to, say no. And remember, 'no' can be a complete sentence (or perhaps 'no, sorry' or 'no, but thank you'. You don't always have to give a reason or an excuse.

So many people have trouble saying 'no' to people, but it's important in terms of our own personal boundaries. And, guess what? Just as with everything else in life, the more we exercise our 'no' muscle, the easier it becomes to keep saying no.

128.

Today, say yes to something you don't usually say yes to (unless, of course, you really don't want to do it, in which case, perhaps repeat yesterday's prompt instead!).

For instance, if your friend is always trying to get you to go out for a drink but you always say you're too busy or you don't have the time, perhaps – just this once – go for that drink. You never know; you might have a great time, you might learn something, you might feel uplifted by your friend's company, and you might feel relaxed or recharged afterwards.

Again, this prompt very much depends on your situation and your circumstances (and the types of questions/requests you receive!). Don't say yes to something you absolutely hate, but do say yes if you're on the fence or have been putting something off that you do actually want to do. You never know where that 'yes' could lead.

129.

Treat your nose. Yep, you read that right. Today, buy something or use something you already have to pamper your nostrils.

Use a room spray you usually forget you have, go and treat yourself to a bottle of your favourite perfume, get some flowers for your bedroom, or try out some new body spray or shower gel. Buy a new diffuser or light a candle, or get some of those wax melts you use over a tea light. Or perhaps just make yourself a lovely smelling herbal tea – fruit teas always smell delicious.

Just get something that smells amazing, and treat your nose!

Personally, I'm a big fan of room sprays and wax melts, especially in the autumn and winter when all the fall scents and Christmas sprays get released. I have a particularly amazing room spray called 'homemade cookie' that smells incredible, and I have lots of apple cider, sugar cookie, and pumpkin wax melts. Pure heaven!

130.

Get your notebook and write out the following:

I am grateful for the sun.

Then, read it back to yourself – out loud – several times, and look out at the sun. OK, if it's night, this won't work, and don't look directly at the sun for too long, but make sure you appreciate everything it does for us. Without it, there'd be no life on this planet. That's pretty huge.

We often forget the little things we should be grateful for, and writing them down and saying them out loud can help us remember.

131.

Make yourself (and perhaps your family or friends) your favourite meal. You know, the meal you'd request if you were ever – God forbid – on death row and it was your last night. Make sure you do it with your favourite sides, drinks, and dessert, and enjoy every single bite.

The truth is, most of us don't know when our last day on earth will be, so we don't know when our last meal will be. Imagine if you died never having had your favourite meal again? Terrible! So, get that eaten today, and if you can share it with people you love, do that too (especially if cooking for and nourishing your friends and family is your 'love language'). Share the food, share the love.

132.

Take a pen and paper and write out the following sentence three times. Then read it back to yourself, out loud, and make sure you mean every word:

"I am so incredibly lucky for everything I have in my life. Just the fact that I am reading these words – that I have the ability to read and that I had the money to purchase this book – makes me so incredibly lucky. I am blessed."

That's it.

When listing our blessings, it's so easy to forget the 'obvious' things, like having the ability to read and write, but even today so many people in the world do not have these basic skills. We are so, so lucky.

133.

Start laughing. Right now. Think of something funny – your favourite comedy scene in a movie, something hilarious that happened in your life recently, a meme or GIF you enjoyed… whatever gets you there.

Then just keep laughing. Sometimes, the more we laugh – even at nothing – the more we want to continue laughing, and laughing is good for the soul.

Of course, laughing therapy is a thing, and sometimes even just watching people do this is enough to get you laughing. Try looking up a clip on YouTube and see if it works for you. After all, I think we can all agree, life is pretty damn weird and pretty damn funny a lot of the time.

134.

Imagine there's a rule that, in your last moments on earth, you get to utter just one sentence, and you have to pick one out of the following (I know, weird rule, right?). You can only say one, and you can't lie. Which sentence would you rather hear coming out of your mouth just before you passed on?

Yep, it's another morbid one, folks. Here are the options:

- "I spent all my life wishing I was someone else."
- "I didn't spend nearly enough time just hanging out and having fun with friends and family."
- "I never let limiting beliefs or fear stand in my way – I went out there and I tried everything and anything."
- "I wished I'd spent more time going after my dreams."
- "I wished I'd spent less time working and more time relaxing."
- "I had so many places I wanted to visit, and I barely got to see any of them."
- "I did everything with as much love, grace, and kindness as I could."
- "I regret nothing."
- "I had so much more that I wanted to achieve."
- "Life has been good to me."
- "Life has kicked my ass."

- "I grabbed life by the hands (or balls, whatever works for you) and I didn't let go the whole time."

You can also add your own sentences. The point is, which of these will be true when the time comes? And are you OK with that or not? Different strokes for different folks means that what's right for one person won't be right for the next, so really think about this and what applies to your own life, rather than what you think the 'correct' answer should be.

135.

Grab your notebook and write out your definition of 'love'. What does it mean to you? How do you show it? How do the people in your life show it to you? What does it involve? What does it feel like? How often do you feel it?

Most of us never take the time to put into words what certain terms – such as 'love' – actually mean to us, and doing so can really make us look at our lives, our circumstances, and the people we surround ourselves with in a new light. It can make us feel grateful, as well as showing us how we can express certain things in better ways.

136.

This is a bit morbid, but it's for a good reason!

Close your eyes and imagine your life without your partner, your parents, your children, your sibling, or your best friend (just pick one).

What would it look like on a daily basis? What would be different about it? What things would you miss the most? Being able to talk to them about your problems? Being able to phone them and chat about anything and everything? Seeing their smile light up their face? Just hanging out?

Then, open your eyes and write down all those things, really taking a moment to feel incredibly grateful that you have that person in your life.

As a second part of the exercise, imagine that person is gone and think of what you'd wish you could say to them. Write it down – and then (you know what I'm going to say), either pick up the phone or message them, saying that exact thing. Just make sure to rewrite it a bit if you need to (so it doesn't sound like they're dead!).

For instance, you might tell that person that you love them, you appreciate them, you enjoy spending time with them, you're grateful for the ways they help you, and so on. It might also include a compliment, something you've often admired about that person but have perhaps never told them before. A lot of the time, we never say these things to the other person, and one day, it could be too late. Don't let that happen.

137.

Get your notebook and write out the following:

I am grateful for the plumbing I have in my house.

Read it back to yourself – out loud – several times, and then really think about this for a moment. Even people who have regular gratitude practices might not list 'plumbing' as something they're grateful for every day, but so many people don't have this luxury, and it sure makes our lives a lot easier.

We often forget the little things we should be grateful for, and writing them down and saying them out loud can help us remember.

138.

Not so long ago, the average lifespan of a human was a lot shorter than it is today. Many people didn't even live to see 40.

So, just think for a moment: if you knew the average lifespan of a human was 40 years old (and if you're over 40, just pretend you're younger for this exercise), would it change the way you lived your life? Would you do anything differently? Would you fast-track certain things to make sure you got it done in time?

Write out five ideas of things you would do differently, for instance:

1. I would definitely exercise more in an attempt to lengthen my lifespan, and eat as well as I could.

2. I would surround myself with people I loved and who encouraged me and supported me, and cut out all the Negative Nellies.

3. I would not put off that trip of a lifetime. I'd find a way to do it in the next few months.

4. I would do less of the things I felt I 'should' do, and more of the things I actually wanted to do.

5. If I'm being really honest, despite the healthy eating, I would also – occasionally – eat a lot more cake while I still could.

We all think we have so many years left on this planet, and many young people act as if they're never going to die. This exercise gets you thinking about what's most important in life, and you can apply the things on your list to your life even though the lifespan (thankfully) isn't 40 years anymore.

139.

Help a neighbour. Do you live near an elderly person or someone who can't leave the house much due to medical reasons? Can you offer to help them in some way? Get them something from the shop? Mow their lawn? Clean their kitchen? Just sit and have a cup of tea and a chat with them? Even if they say no, go and offer.

If you don't know them very well (or don't know of anyone local you could help), try posting on a community forum or in a Facebook group, asking if anyone needs help with anything. You never know who may be in need.

You could also ask friends and family if any of their neighbours need help, or if they know of anyone who would benefit from a trip to the shops or a lift to the bank, or whatever it might be. It's worth an ask.

140.

Here's a thinker. Imagine that you're stuck in a version of *Groundhog Day*, and that you knew tomorrow was going to be exactly the same as today (and the day after that, and the day after that), in every way, apart from one thing – one thing you could choose to change. What would you change?

Would you get out the house for a walk if you've spent all day inside? Would you pick up the phone and call someone you haven't spoken to in ages? Would you make sure you had a giant chocolate cake in the house, ready to eat? What would you do if you could only change one thing? It's a toughie.

141.

'Get better sleep' prompt: Wear an eye mask to bed.

Blocking out light from your room can help you get better sleep, especially if you have even the slightest bit of light coming in through your curtains or if you have electronic devices nearby with standby lights on. Remember: sleep is so incredibly important, so anything you can do to minimise distractions and help you get a better night's sleep is well worth doing.

142.

Grab your notebook and write out your definition of 'wealth'. What does it mean to you? What different types of wealth are there? Do you feel wealthy in general? Or is it something you're striving for? What do you think it will feel like when you get there?

Of course, often, the first thing we think when we hear the word 'wealth' is money, but we can be wealthy in so many different ways. So, what does wealth mean to you?

143.

Fix something you've been meaning to fix. Tackle that wonky shelf or the door that creaks in your house. Darn a sock (do people still do that?). Sort out that kitchen drawer that keeps sticking. Change that lightbulb you've been meaning to change for weeks.

If it's something you don't know how to fix yourself, Google how to do it or ask someone else to fix it for you. If you rent and the something that needs fixing is in the house, ask your landlord to sort it out.

Fixing even little things in our lives can give us great satisfaction, and guess what? If we start fixing the little things, we can then graduate to fixing the big things, and before long, we're fixing everything we dislike about our lives.

144.

Be a bit whacky and celebrate a holiday on a different day to usual (or at least a bit of it if you don't want to go all out).

Love Christmas? Make today Fake Christmas Day and down some eggnog. Give your partner a Valentine's gift even if it isn't Valentine's Day. Celebrate the New Year and make a list of things you want to achieve over the next 12 months, whether it's January or not. The calendar doesn't have to dictate what you do when! Go on, it's fun!

Christmas. Valentine's. New Year's Eve. St Patrick's Day. Thanksgiving. Fourth of July. Easter. Halloween. Bonfire Night. Mix and match with other country's holidays if you wish. After all, many countries all around the world celebrate St. Patrick's Day! So, why not mix things up a bit and celebrate your favourite holiday today?

145.

Check out the powerhouse of a woman that is Marie Forleo. She's cool, she's feisty, and she's been called 'a thought leader for the next generation' by Oprah.

Not only does she have hundreds of amazing free MarieTV episodes available for you to view – all about business, self-development, and kicking ass in general – but she's also written an awesome book, *Everything Is Figureoutable*, as well as running B-School, an annual online business school that teaches the modern entrepreneur everything they need to know to build a successful purpose-driven business from a place of sincerity and honesty.

I'm a proud B-School alumnus, and my business wouldn't be the business it is today if I hadn't gone through that programme.

146.

If the weather's nice, go to a local meadow, field, park, or bit of grass (or in your garden if you have one), and have a bit of a frolic.

Yes, you heard me right. Frolic.

Run around and jump and smile and just pretend you're a kid again, with nothing else to do but have a nice frolic in a field.

If you feel stupid doing this on your own, and you have a friend or family member who doesn't mind being a bit silly, ask them to have a frolic with you. It's probably more fun with other people anyway. Hell, have a frolic party! Find a hill and roll down it, go crazy! Life is short!

Yes, this is a weird one, but have you ever had a proper frolic in the grass? It's pretty awesome.

147.

Make your bed.

Yes, it's a nice simple one today.

If you already make your bed every day, give yourself a pat on the back and bask in your awesomeness. So many successful people say that their success starts with making their bed first thing in the morning.

You're taking action, you're bringing order to your life, and it just looks better once it's done. It's all about keeping organised and staying consistent, doing it every day. If you can do that one task every day and keep it up for months or years, you can do the same thing with any other task you need to complete, until it becomes a habit.

If you already do this, why not mix it up a bit? Try some different bedding or add some extra pillows to make your bed look a little more stylish. Pimp that bed-making routine!

148.

Today, choose to be happy. Choose to be positive. Choose to smile. Choose to see the good things in life. Choose to be thankful for your blessings. Choose to enjoy – or at least feel grateful for – every moment you get to be alive on this crazy, wonderful planet.

Just choose. Often, it's as simple as that.

149.

Grab your notebook and write out your definition of 'contentment'. What does it mean to you? What does it feel like? What things make you feel content? Do you generally feel content in life or not? Do you wish you felt more content? What do you think would change your level of contentment?

'Content' is defined as being in a 'state of peaceful happiness' (according to Oxford Languages, as shown in the Google results for 'content'). So that's peace AND happiness. What makes you feel like this?

150.

Take a dull, boring object from your house and make it beautiful (or at least a little more appealing to the eye).

Paint it, bling it up, repurpose it, polish it, whatever. Just breathe life back into the poor old thing. This could be an old piece of furniture that you upcycle, a doorknob that needs polishing, or a table that you can cover in an attractive tablecloth. It doesn't have to be rocket science.

And, if you can do this with an object, guess what? You can do it with your life too!

151.

'Get better sleep' prompt: Use a pillow spray, like a nice lavender one.

Lavender is such a relaxing scent, and spraying it on your pillow or your clothes can really help relax both your body and your mind. Remember: sleep is so incredibly important, so anything you can do to minimise distractions and help you get a better night's sleep is well worth doing.

152.

Give yourself – or a loved one – a 'micro makeover'.

Try a different hair product or a different brand of make-up, go to the store and try a perfume sample, put on eyeliner or mascara if you don't usually use them, wear a necklace if you don't usually bother with jewellery, and so on.

One tiny thing is all I'm asking for, but feel free to do more if you want. Dye your hair a different shade. Try some stick-on nails, or stick-on earrings if you don't have your ears pierced. Try a temporary tattoo or get a henna tattoo… the list is endless!

I know not everyone is particularly interested in make-up or getting their hair done, but even a tiny thing like painting your nails or using a different hair gel can be enough to pull you out of that same old rut and routine of getting ready every day. And if you're not into it, ask a friend or family member if they want a micro makeover.

153.

Get some friends together – or your kids, or whoever – and dress up, whether you have anywhere to go or not.

Dress up fancy, or dress up in fancy dress. Just do something different, and have a little fun. You can take pictures when you're done, or maybe swap an outfit with a friend. Life's too short not to be silly occasionally.

If you're not into fancy dress (or dressing fancy), just keep it simple. Get some pointy ears, do some over the top make-up, or don a bright wig. Just wear something a little out of the norm, even if there's no particular reason for it. Why not?

154.

If you had to come up with a business/side hustle idea on the spot, right now, what would it be? Write it down and come up with a few details.

Now, is this something you could actually start? Or perhaps just make into a hobby? If it came to mind, it's probably something you're passionate about, or at least vaguely interested in.

Whether you have a dream of starting your own business or not, this can be an interesting exercise – I bet you have more ideas than you might think, and more skills, talent, and knowledge about certain topics than you realise.

155.

If it's nice weather, put a picnic together and go and eat outside for a change (if you don't generally do this).

Invite a friend and take a blanket, a picnic basket, some nutritious food (and some tasty treats), and perhaps a bottle of something to share. Turn off your phones and other devices and just enjoy it.

It's nice to do something different, and if the weather's on your side, it can be a nice break from the indoors and from your screens.

It doesn't have to be anything fancy. If you don't have a picnic blanket and basket, take any old blanket or scarf to sit on, or find somewhere that has picnic benches. You don't have to spend hours putting together an epic feast, either; it could just be a sandwich, a drink, and a packet of crisps from the shop.

156.

Write out the following sentence:

"It doesn't matter what happens to me. What matters is how I react to it."

Then read it out loud to yourself a few times, mulling it over in your mind. Do you agree with this? Can you give any examples from your own life?

Of course, some things happen to you and they're just terrible, and there might not be many different ways to react to it. Generally, however, we can choose how we react to something – to someone yelling at us or talking about us behind our backs, to something going wrong at work, and so on. As you go through life, it doesn't matter what happens to you. What matters is how you react to it.

157.

Do an audit of your life. Take each part of your life – job/career, love life, home life, family, friends, hobbies, ambitions – and write down anything you're not happy with.

Look at your life from the outside in, like an auditor would look at someone's company/business. Try to detach yourself emotionally from your life when completing this task, so that you can really get down to the nitty gritty of anything that's not working.

Once you have this list, put it up in a place where you'll see it regularly, to remind yourself of what you want to work on.

Sometimes, we might not even be aware of the things we're not happy with in our lives until we sit down and do this kind of exercise – or we might know that some things are wrong, but be unable to pinpoint exactly what those things are. This exercise can help.

158.

Get your workout clothes on, head to YouTube, and find a fun dance workout to try.

There are so many available on there these days, set to all sorts of music, so find a music genre you enjoy and try one of those.

It's good for your physical health, and it's also good for your mental health – especially if the song you're dancing to is upbeat and motivational. Do it alone or try it with a friend, and get those endorphins flowing!

This can be a great way to get some exercise in a fun way. Going to the gym or going for a run can feel too much like exercise, if that makes sense, but dancing around to music you love and learning a routine can be really fun. And don't worry about looking stupid – everyone looks stupid at the start, and that's part of the fun too. If you really feel self-conscious, just do the video alone and make sure your curtains are closed. Before long I'm sure you'll be killing that routine without caring who might see you!

159.

Go camping for a night, even if it's just in your back garden/backyard (as long as it's not absolutely freezing and there's no horrendous weather forecast).

This is all about switching up your environment and doing something different. Do it with a partner, a friend, or your kids, and make it into a fun adventure.

If you're not into camping at all (and I have to say, I put myself firmly in this camp – rubbish pun intended) then just pop outside for a bit in the evening, wrapped up warm if needed, and lie down and look at the stars if you're able.

Just take some time to reconnect with the world and remind yourself how vast the universe really is. It's incredible.

If you live in the middle of a city and have no outdoor space of your own, I admit this will be tricky. But you can always improvise – 'camp' in your living room, pretending to be sitting around a campfire. You could even use those glow-in-the-dark stars on your ceiling, or string up some fairy lights to represent the stars. Kids will love this, but big kids can get just as much of a kick out of it, so give it a go.

160.

Reframe your mindset around: fear.

I talk about this a lot in my *Write Your Life* book, and it's something many of us have to constantly work on.

Fear is good for us – as long as we keep it in check and don't let it walk all over us – so don't try to avoid it. Instead, make it your best friend. Fear is the original frenemy, and what are we told to do? Keep our friends close and our enemies closer. Fear will always be with us, a constant companion, but that doesn't mean we need to listen to it all the time.

As I say in my book, fear is just excitement in a fancy hat. Don't let it control you, and don't get confused between things that scare you and things that excite you.

161.

Get a pen and paper and write down the following sentence:

"If it's not a hell yes, it's a hell no!"

Read it back over a few times, out loud, and shout it out if necessary. This is from the highly successful Marie Forleo, though many people have said similar versions of this sentence.

Then, whenever anyone asks you to do something or you have a decision to make, say that sentence to yourself again before responding. If you're not immediately thinking 'hell yes!', then it's a 'hell no'.

Of course, there are some instances when things will be a little more complicated, such as when someone who really needs assistance asks you to help them out. If you're busy and don't think you have the time, your initial response might not be a 'hell yes' but more of an 'ehhh, I should probably help them out'. So, take it each circumstance at a time, but use this sentence as a benchmark.

162.

Grab your notebook and write out your definition of 'achievement'. What does it mean to you? What immediately comes to mind when you hear that word? What does achievement feel like to you?

The word 'achievement' can apply to many different things. Achievement at work, in your personal life, in sports, at home… it can apply to awards and reviews, monetary gain, and a hundred other things. So, what does it mean to you? Write it all out.

163.

Get your creative juices flowing and design a movie poster for your life.

You can use free software like Canva to do it, or any other program you have on your computer – or you can draw it yourself on paper.

Take your life as it is now, today. What genre would your life be as a movie? What title would you give it? What image would you use? What tag line? Would it be an epic adventure or a subdued drama? A comedy? A romcom? A tragedy, perhaps? A bright, bold musical or a dark, chilling horror?

Then, once you've got your poster, I want you to make another one – this one for the life you want to have, your dream life. How would the genre change? The title? The image? The tag line? Compare the two and perhaps put them up on your wall as something to aim for.

I love this one! It can be a really great exercise as it's fun, it's creative, and it gets you thinking about your own life and how you'd like it to be. You could even put the finished product out on social media and suggest that your friends and family try doing it too, or you could get together with a bunch of friends and come up with your movie posters together.

164.

Right before you go to bed, take a notepad and pen and do a 'brain dump' of everything you're currently worried about or feeling anxious about.

Scribble it all out – it doesn't have to be amazing handwriting or proper sentences – and get it all down on paper. Then, as you lie down and go to sleep you'll feel much lighter, having poured out all your problems onto the page.

This can be a good thing to do every single night before you head to bed, and the more you get into the habit, the easier it will become to let go of these things and have a good night's rest.

Sleep is everything, so don't waste any of those precious hours in bed tossing and turning and worrying about things. Get them down on paper and then relax, safe in the knowledge that you've already given some thought to the things bothering you. Hey, you never know, your subconscious might even work on your problems during the night and present you with a solution in the morning (or via your dreams!).

165.

Here's another writing exercise for you. Think back to when you were a child. Can you remember wishing that your life was different at any point (even if it was only briefly, perhaps after a fight with your parents or after an incident at school)?

Did you wish you'd been born in another country or had grown up in a different place? Did you wish your family was richer, or closer, or did more things together? Did you dream about growing up in a bigger house, with more material items and more family holidays?

Whatever it was, write it all down, then ask yourself: if you'd had what you'd wanted as a child, where do you think you'd be now? Would you be living somewhere else, doing something else? Would you be happier or not? Would you prefer that life or this one?

Be honest here, and don't worry – there are no right or wrong answers to this. It's just a way of showing you that you either have a different life in mind that you'd like to work towards, or that you're happy with how things worked out and happy with where you are now, in which case, you can be thankful for your lot in life. Write out that gratitude in your notebook and feel every word of it.

166.

Let out your inner child and build a blanket or pillow fort in your home.

Tie blankets to chairs, sofas, and tables, and get creative with how you 'decorate' your blanket fort inside. I recommend fairy lights and battery-powered candles, to really make it a nice place to hang out.

Then, just chill in there for a while, away from the world and away from your TV, games console, or computer. Just be quiet and think. Or – if you're doing this with others – get talking or put some music on and have a party.

Personally, I seem to collect blankets and cushions, so creating a blanket/cushion fort would be easy for me. If you're not a soft furnishings hoarder, you might need to borrow some items from your friends or family – though be warned: they might want an invite too!

167.

'Get better sleep' prompt: Stop using electronic devices right before bed – phones, tablets, e-readers, computers… anything that emits blue light.

I'm sure we're all guilty of this, especially with regards to scrolling through websites and social media feeds on our phone when we're actually in bed. Unfortunately, it doesn't help with sleep at all. Remember: sleep is so incredibly important, so anything you can do to minimise distractions and help you get a better night's sleep is well worth doing.

168.

Take some time out for yourself and do some meditation. If you've never tried it before, look for videos online or download an app such as Headspace or Calm.

To start, just try it for a few minutes – you can always build up the duration later, if you decide to carry on with the practice. You can meditate on a certain thought – such as a problem or issue you want to solve – or you can just use the time to clear your mind and ground yourself.

As with anything worth doing, meditation can take a while to get used to, and if you want to continue with it you'll have to practice and find out what works best for you. YouTube and meditation apps are a great place to start.

169.

Make a plan to back up your life – and your mind – just like you'd back up your computer with an external hard drive or your photos in the cloud.

Basically, this is all about making sure that your most important memories, lessons learnt, achievements, and so on get 'backed up' somewhere, so even if something happens to you (or your memory), those things will be safe. But how on earth do you go about doing something like this? Well, there are several options:

• Write a book (or get someone else to write a book from the information you give them). This could be an autobiography, a memoir, or a novel – a fictionalised version of your life. (Check out my book *Write Your Life: The Ultimate Life Hack For Achieving Your Dreams* for more info on how to start this).

• Start a blog, writing regular articles on things you've done in the past and the lessons you've learnt from them.

• Start a YouTube channel, making videos instead of writing articles.

• Start a Facebook page or an Instagram profile, where you can share your life lessons and memories.

• Keep a diary/journal, with the aim of passing it down to the next generation of your family (or anyone else you know) once it's full, at which point you can start another one.

• Tell other people your stories – have face-to-face conversations with family members or write them out in a letter for your friends and family. Encourage them to tell their friends and family members too, both now and in the future, to make sure your stories get passed on over the years to come.

• Keep a box full of 'life souvenirs', which you can pass down to family/friends. Personally, I have a huge chest full of travelling souvenirs, postcards, tourist brochures, gig tickets, theatre programmes, photos, and anything else I've kept from my travels and days out. If anyone found that chest, they'd instantly be able to understand a lot about me and my life.

Many of us worry about forgetting things from our youth as we get older, of memories slipping past us as we age, and then there's the terrifying thought of everything in our brain – our thoughts, our memories, our achievements – completely vanishing once we've left this earth. A horrible notion. Well, if you back up your life and back up your mind, you can rest easy, safe in the knowledge that you've passed on all the important bits from your time on this planet. Pretty neat, right?

170.

Do you have a specific dream you're striving for above all others? If so, pick a mental image to represent that dream and, every night – when you're in bed and feeling drowsy – run that mental image through your mind several times. Visualise every little bit of it, and make sure it's the same every time.

For instance, you could visualise:

• Someone giving you a promotion at work

- Receiving an award for something

- Crossing the finish line of a marathon

- Fitting into your 'goal dress' if you're getting fit and healthy

- Getting married to the person of your dreams

- Picking up the key and stepping inside your dream home for the first time

- And so on!

You can do this exercise during the day as well – when you're meditating, for example – but doing it before bed every night allows you to develop a habit you're more likely to stick to. If you visualise it while already drowsy, your subconscious mind will get to work on this image while you're sleeping, and perhaps you'll dream about it, or wake up with a new idea for how to achieve it. Your mind is a wonderful thing, so make sure you use it!

171.

Think back to when you were a child, and any irrational fears you had. Did you worry about there being a monster under your bed? Or perhaps in the closet? Were you scared that your house might be full of ghosts? Or that there were zombies or vampires waiting for you in the shadows? I'm sure you can think of something similar.

Can you admit to yourself that these fears were silly, unfounded, and not based on fact? (Unless, of course, you still believe in ghosts and think your house is haunted. And I'm very much into spooky things, so I'm not judging here!).

Now, think of any current fears you have. When you really think about them, are any of these just as silly and unfounded as your childhood fears? Are they based on fact or not? Can you throw them away just like you threw away your childhood fears as you got older?

After all, people change, and their fears change too. Do you think you'll still have the same fears in 10, twenty, thirty years' time? No? Then get rid of them! They're not helping you.

Fears are strange things, but they only have the power we give them, so let's stop giving them power.

172.

Grab your notebook and write out your definition of 'failure'. What does it mean to you? What does it feel like to fail? What failures do you feel have defined you and your journey in the past? Can you agree that, without these failures, you wouldn't be where you are now? With the knowledge you have know? Redefine your notion of failure as being something good that needs to happen in order for you to learn and grow.

As Will Smith says, fail early, fail often, fail forward. We need to fail. If we never failed at anything, we'd never learn the lessons we need to learn to become the best versions of ourselves.

173.

Celebrate being alive!

That's right. I want you to take a moment out of your busy day and simply sit and be thankful for the fact that you're even alive and breathing, living on this planet, right now. So many people aren't. So many people only got a few years on this earth before they were ripped away from life, and some got even less.

We lost so many souls during the pandemic, and we're still losing so many people every day due to a million different things. Be happy and grateful that you are alive right now. Celebrate it. You're one of the lucky ones.

You can celebrate in any way you want. Have a drink, treat yourself to something nice, have a long phone conversation with someone you love, have a dance, or simply sit and be thankful. Ideally, this is something we should be doing every day – as every day is a gift – but just today will do for now.

174.

Here's a basic prompt for you: Cut down on your sugar intake.

Sugar is the devil! OK, so maybe that's going a bit far, but it is bad for us in so many ways, so cutting down on it can only help.

Cut out sugar in your tea or coffee, cut down on the sugary Starbucks-style drinks, the same with pop (or soda, depending on where you're from), and then the usual suspects such as chocolate, biscuits, cakes, ice cream, and so on.

Obviously, treating yourself occasionally is not only allowed but needed (in my opinion), but just for today, try to reduce your sugar intake.

And be aware that sugar is in almost everything, especially processed foods. Just take a while to look at the labels on the things in your fridge and cupboards.

175.

What season are you in right now? (And I don't mean the four divisions of the year, although we can still refer to our own personal seasons with those names.)

For instance, are you in a frantic summer season, full of light and warmth and energy? Or are you feeling cold, tired, and lethargic, like you're stuck in a perpetual winter? Perhaps you're somewhere in between, in an autumn season of winding down, or perhaps you're just blossoming into your spring season, getting ready to ramp up your work and your energy. We go through different seasons all the time, and they don't always correspond with the actual seasons.

Write down what season you're in currently, describing why you feel that way, and then write down which season you want to be in/which one you're working towards, and how you're going to achieve that.

Recognising what season we're currently in can really help us, especially if we're being hard on ourselves for not getting enough done. If you're currently in your winter season, not getting much done and feeling tired and lethargic, it might be because you've just come out of a busy summer season, where you worked hard, played hard, and used up a lot of energy. You might have burned yourself out a little bit, hence needing a winter season of more rest and relaxation before you 'spring' into life when you get your energy back. Understanding where we are and where we're heading can make all the difference.

176.

Today, turn off your phone for an hour or two (unless you're waiting for an important call or need to keep the line open in case of emergency).

If you're always on your phone, this can be difficult, but it can also be SO freeing. You can get so much more done when you're not being constantly distracted by phone calls, texts, and internet notifications, and it will give your brain and your eyesight a break too. If you can, do it for more than an hour or two, and see how it goes.

Try this exercise with other devices too: tablets, computers, and anything else electronic that is constantly vying for your attention. Sometimes, we all just need a bit of a break.

177.

Get out your notebook or computer and write a review – a review of your life so far. As if it were a movie or a book.

- How many stars would you give it?
- What genre would you say it is?
- What have the highlights been so far?
- What were the worst bits?
- Could anything be improved?
- Would you recommend it to others?

Yes, this can seem a little silly, but it's yet another way of looking at our lives from a different perspective. And, if you haven't given your life five stars, and if you can honestly say you wouldn't recommend it to others, it might be time to start changing some things – possibly some major things.

You don't have to be one of those horrible, impossible-to-please critics with this exercise. Just be honest about your life, and cut yourself some slack. We've all had bad things happen in our lives, and we all have things we can improve on. This is meant to be a fun exercise, so don't take it too seriously.

178.

Make a list of everything that makes you feel truly alive, even if you've only ever done it once in your life. They can be big things or little things. For instance:

- Jumping out of a plane (skydiving, not just general jumping)
- Singing on stage or just being on stage in front of an audience

- Going for a walk in nature

- Going camping and sleeping beneath the stars

- Hanging out with friends in a pub/bar and just chatting and laughing, without a care in the world

- Following your passion, whatever that might be

Then, do one of them! Or at least make a plan to do one of them soon if they're all 'big' things. Life is too short to not feel truly alive on a regular basis.

179.

Here's a basic prompt for you: Do more exercise today!

Even if you exercise regularly, we all know how great it is for our body, our mindset, and our mood, so see if you can add on an extra 10-20 minutes today.

So many people think exercise is boring, but you just need to find something you enjoy. Walking, dancing to music, fitness videos, team sports, running, going to the gym, swimming, joining a dance class… there are so many ways to exercise!

180.

What are you excited about in your life right now? Are you looking forward to a holiday you've booked? Are you excited to see a friend you haven't seen in a long time? Perhaps you have a birthday coming up or some other kind of celebration? It could even be a little thing, like being excited about redecorating your living room, or picking out a paint colour for your bedroom.

Whatever it is, write it down and then tell someone! Tell the people you live with (if you live with anyone), tell your friends and family, tell people on social media or in a WhatsApp group. Then ask them what they're excited about right now. Get excited together! Celebrate your excitement! Woop!

If you're excited about something in life, celebrate it! So many people would kill to have something to be excited about in their lives, to have something to look forward to. It really is a gift, and one we don't really think about much.

181.

Send someone in your life a cute handwritten note or card to let them know you're thinking of them. It doesn't have to be anything special – just send them a physical card rather than a text or an email. Sometimes, it's nice to go old school.

I think everyone appreciates the thought and time that goes into actually sending something physical in the post these days, but older people might appreciate it more, especially if they don't regularly use a computer or a phone. Just send them a little something to make them smile; I'm sure it will make you smile too.

182.

Today, change your walk. And I'm not talking 'Ministry of Silly Walks' here, though please feel free to go down that route if you wish! I'm talking about putting some pep in your step, upping your energy, and feeling great.

If we walk around slowly, all hunched over and staring at the ground, we're going to feel pretty crappy. If we walk around with our back straight, our head held high, our chest out, and with a happy, confident energy about us, we're going to feel great – and it might rub off on other people too.

I always think of the Amazon show, *The Marvelous Mrs. Maisel*; whenever she's about to go on stage to perform her stand-up routine, she and her manager say 'Tits up!' and she straightens her posture, ready to slay it on stage. It works.

So go ahead: change your walk, and see how your outlook changes.

By putting out a more confident, happy vibe when you're walking around, you'll probably see other people reacting to you in a different way too. They might smile at you more, or try to talk to you, or even feel energised by the awesome vibes you're putting out there. This works well in work environments, such as when you're walking into a room to give a presentation, but it can also help in other areas of life too.

183.

If you use any kind of notes app in your phone, take a moment to sort it out and get your notes organised. I use mine all the time, and if I don't stay on top of them, my notes get out of control.

Go through them, deleting the ones you no longer need, and prioritising them if required. I use Google Keep, which I love because you can give your notes labels, you can colour-code them, and you can pin the important ones to the top of the app screen. Plus, it just looks pretty.

This might seem like a rather small thing to do, but if you can keep your phone organised, you can keep your life organised – it's just about taking the time to sort through things, and staying consistent. And, if you don't use a notes app on your phone, think about giving it a go – it's super handy.

184.

American football player Lou Holtz said, "If you're bored with life—you don't get up every morning with a burning desire to do things—you don't have enough goals."

Do you get up every morning with a burning desire to do something? Or are you on the 'bored with life' side?

Figure out what side you're on now and what side you'd like to be on.

Then make a plan to do something about it!

185.

Grab your notebook and write out your definition of 'courage'. What does it mean to you? What does it feel like to have courage? To be courageous? How do you see other people illustrating courage? In which areas of your life do you wish you had more courage? And what could you do to get it (and I'm not talking Dutch courage here)? Not everyone defines this in the same way, so see what you come up with.

Remember that we don't have to be completely courageous all the time, and it's OK not to feel courageous even if you think you should. Sometimes, we have to build up our courage muscle for a certain situation over time, and that's totally fine.

186.

If you're tired of journalling or writing things down, why not take a break from the pen or the keyboard and use your voice?

Record yourself on your phone, send yourself voice notes, or use a dictation programme to talk into a Word document. Voice notes in particular are a great way to get your thoughts out without having to stop, sit down, and start writing. You can do it as you're going around the house, getting ready for the day, or when you're out walking.

It might seem a little strange 'talking to yourself' at first, but as with anything, the more you do it, the more comfortable you'll be doing it.

187.

If you can't get outside your house today for a walk (or any day where there are time limitations or weather limitations), walk around your house instead. If you can put on some upbeat music, even better.

Yes, it might not be as nice as going for a walk in nature, but if you power walk and do it to music, it can still get your heart rate up and be a good workout. Plus, the music might get you motivated for all the other things you need to do.

Even if you have a small house, you can still do this. Walk from your living room to your kitchen, or up and down your stairs if you have them, or wherever you can. You can even march on the spot if you really don't have much space. Get creative!

188.

Find your favourite motivational quotes online (Google them, you'll find hundreds!) and then record a few in your own voice, saving them to your phone.

Then, play them back to yourself every morning, or whenever you need an additional boost.

Reading motivational quotes is all well and good, but hearing them in your own voice is even better. It's a great way of motivating yourself!

189.

Is there an embarrassing moment from your past that tends to 'haunt' you? You know, you'll be having a perfectly lovely day and then the memory of that thing will rear its ugly head out of nowhere and make you cringe.

Well, is there any way you could reframe that memory? See it from someone else's perspective? Laugh at yourself? See the funny side? Sometimes, all it takes is time; something that embarrassed you when you were younger might seem like nothing when you're older and have been through so many other things. Take a few minutes to see how you could reframe that moment in your mind, and then write down how you did it.

I don't know about you, but I have several of these moments, and they don't have to be big things – sometimes, just tiny moments stick in our minds because of how they made us feel, while we can forget lots of other moments where we didn't feel such an extreme emotion. Thanks, brain!

190.

Grab your notebook and write out your definition of 'confidence'. What does it mean to you? What does it feel like to have confidence? To *be* confident? In which areas of your life do you feel most confident? Where do you wish you had more confidence? What can you do to gain confidence? Journal on it and get all your thoughts down on the page.

Here's a hint: confidence comes from action, not from thought. Yes, mindset is everything, but if you're not feeling confident about a particular area of your life, the way to gain confidence is to get out there and do the thing you're worried about. Don't think, 'Once I'm fitter and healthier and slimmer, I will be more confident.' Go out and do the regular exercise – it is *that* which will make you confident. Confidence comes through action and progress.

191.

Finances. Yes, that's right – that scary word. If you're anything like me, you might find this subject puzzling to say the least. If you do, I'd like to introduce you to Robert T. Kiyosaki.

If you want to learn about finance (and a load of other stuff), this guy certainly knows what he's talking about. I particularly recommend his book *Rich Dad Poor Dad*, which – as his website says – is the number one personal finance book of all time. It's a really interesting read, and it will make you think about money, assets, and liabilities in a completely new way.

For today, add this book to your reading list and/or take a look at his site: www.richdad.com.

192.

Here's another writing exercise. If you had to go back to the first day of high school, knowing everything you know now, would you do anything differently?

Would you make different friends? Choose different subjects? Join different clubs? Try out different hobbies? Hang out in different places after school?

Write out a paragraph or two describing what you'd change and why.

High school, for a lot of us, is where we really come into our own as individuals. We learn what we like and what we don't like (and who we like and don't like), we start formulating our plans and dreams for the future, and the experiences we have during those years shape us in a big way. So, what – if anything – would you change?

193.

Breathe. That's right, I want you to breathe. We rarely take the time to focus on our breathing, but it can be so beneficial to sit down for a few minutes and really concentrate on the air we're letting into and out of our lungs.

One easy exercise you can do is to breathe in through your nose for a count of four, hold your breath for a count of four, and then release your breath – this time through your mouth – for a count of eight. Then repeat the whole thing another three or four times. There. Do you feel any better?

Breathing exercises such as these can help us slow down, ground ourself, and really focus on being in the present moment. They can relax us and help return our heart rate to normal. Give it a go – who knows, you might make this into a regular part of your day.

194.

Today I want you to take a moment to think about all the things you enjoy doing (at work and in your spare time), and then make two lists: things you enjoy the pursuit of (the actual process of working towards a specific goal), and then the things you enjoy when you achieve them (the actual moment you successfully achieve the thing).

These are not always the same. For instance, you might really enjoy striving for something – doing all the planning and the groundwork and so on – but when you eventually achieve that thing, it's always a bit anticlimactic or perhaps even a bit disappointing. For example, you might love organising an event but aren't particularly bothered about attending the actual event yourself.

You might also have other tasks where you really enjoy the end goal (such as having a shiny new book published, and all the marketing and networking that comes with it), but find the actual process of writing a book akin to pulling teeth. Fortunately, I don't feel that way, but I know many do.

Write out all the tasks you can think of, then see if there are any overlaps – any at all, no matter how small. Did any activity or task – or any particular aspects of an activity or task – make it into both list 1 and list 2? If so, these are the things you should be focusing on. Be aware of them. Appreciate them. Do them as much as you can.

If they're business-based tasks, see if you can include these more in your own business, or if you work for someone else, ask them if you can do more of these types of tasks and less of the ones that didn't make it onto your 'overlap list' (or the ones that didn't make it onto either of the first two lists!).

This isn't always possible at work, of course, but if you're spending your whole day working on things you hate, that's a whole other subject and a whole other question: Can you find a role more suited to your abilities and the things you actually enjoy doing? It's worth thinking about.

If you're constantly doing things just for the feeling you get when you achieve them, while hating the long, hard slog it takes to get there, you're probably spending a lot of time not enjoying yourself at all, whether it's at work or in your spare time. And, if you're enjoying going after something but then don't enjoy the actual moment when you achieve it, you might want to reconsider if all that work is worth it. For some, it will be totally worth it. For others, they might decide to spend their precious time doing other things, where the outcome is just as exciting as the process. Finding things you enjoy working towards *and* achieving is the goal.

195.

Take some time out to watch Marie Forleo's awesome Oprah SuperSoul Session, Everything Is Figureoutable (available at www.marieforleo.com).

I love Marie, and I love the way she tells her story. Most importantly, though, I love her message – that absolutely everything is figureoutable. So, what do you need figuring out in your life at the moment? Watch the video and get inspired!

And, if you liked that, check out Marie Forleo's amazing book of the same name!

196.

Grab your notebook and write out your definition of 'determination'. What does it mean to you? What does it feel like to have determination? To be determined? In which areas of your life do you feel most determined? Where has your determination got you in the past? What do you need to feel more determination around now? Write down anything and everything that comes to mind.

Do you generally consider yourself a determined person? Or do you look up to others who are? Get it all out and write it all down.

197.

Reframe your mindset around: life.

Yep, the big 'L' word. The truth is, many of us don't think about life in general at all. Unless we're an actual philosopher, we don't spend our days and nights wondering who we are, where we came from, or why we're here.

When you really stop and think about it, life is pretty damn amazing. How awesome is it that we're on this planet, alive, right now? When so many people have died, and so many things could have stopped us from ever even being conceived?

How magic is space? And the fact that we're spinning around in it? The universe is incredible, and we are SO lucky to be here on this planet. Just stop and think about this for a moment, and I mean *really* think about it.

It's even better to think about it when sitting outside, looking up at the stars (if you can see the stars where you live – damn light pollution). I also highly recommend you read *The Solitaire Mystery* by Jostein Gaarder. It's one of my favourite books of all time, and it delves deep into the idea of life and where we come from, all while following a very sweet and entertaining fictional story. I loved it when I was younger, and I still love it to this day.

198.

Do something for yourself today – and just yourself. Take some time to do something you love, on your own, with just yourself for company. And really enjoy it!

For people who live alone, this prompt might not be so dramatic, but if you live in a busy household and never seem to get a moment to yourself, this prompt can mean everything. If the latter is the case for you then this will probably be quite a difficult thing to achieve, but if you try hard enough, I'm sure you could find some time (perhaps first thing in the morning or last thing at night) where you can have a few minutes to yourself to do something you enjoy – without worrying about anyone else.

199.

Help out a local business or someone you know who is self-employed by purchasing one of their products or services, and then share your experience with others (in person, with a review, and so on). You'll feel great, they'll feel great, and hopefully you'll receive a great product or service in return. Win-win!

This doesn't have to be a difficult thing to do, and you don't have to spend a fortune. If you're not sure who to support, or don't know if any of your friends are self-employed/run their own businesses, just ask! Write a post on social media asking who runs their own business (or knows someone who does), and if something takes your fancy, go for it. Local boutiques and independent shops are also an option.

200.

Set some boundaries. I know this is a bit of a vague one, but that's because it's going to be different for different people. For instance, some people need boundaries when it comes to their work, some need them in their relationships, some need them in their home life, and so on.

Setting boundaries can be hard to do at first, but once you have them in place, they can be game-changing. Some examples:

- Someone who works at home might need to set themselves some boundaries, such as when their work day starts and ends, or where they do their work (in their home office only), to keep their work time and personal time separate.

- Someone in a new relationship might need to set boundaries around how much they let their partner 'into' their lives initially, such as if one or both of the people have kids.

- Someone who has their own business and their own clients might need to set boundaries with their clients, informing them that they can only contact them during certain set work hours, and so on.

Boundaries come in all shapes and sizes, and once we start realising how well they work, it gets easier and easier to have the conversation with your partner, friend, colleague, or whoever it is you need to set the boundaries with. Just be upfront about it, and tell them straight: *These are the boundaries I need to set and these are the reasons why I need to set them. Please respect them, and let me know if you have any boundaries you need to set with me, thank you.*

201.

Have a 'movie night' with your best friends.

Sometimes, this is all it takes to lift our mood, relax us, and allow us to set the world to rights. Have a chat, catch up, and then watch something epic and inspiring, or just something funny or thrilling – something you can escape in, for just a couple of hours.

If you don't live near your best friends or if you can't easily meet up in person, do it virtually. Throughout the pandemic I had a weekly virtual movie night with some of my best friends using an app called Teleparty, where you can watch a movie together and chat with each other using a chat box. There are all kinds of ways to have 'watch parties' these days, so check out the options online if you haven't already.

202.

Grab your notebook and write out your definition of 'integrity'. What does it mean to you? What does it feel like to have integrity? In which areas of your life do you think it's most important to have integrity? Do you have it when it comes to every area of your life?

Most of us like to think we have integrity, that we have strong principles and morals that we stick to all the time, and that we're generally honest with other people, but is that true of you, right now? Dig deep and have a really good ponder on this, then journal around what you discover.

203.

If you had to describe your life in one sentence – as if you were describing a book plot, for example – what would you write?

Would it be something like 'A D-student girl from a small town grows up to become a corporate bigwig, proving to everyone who didn't believe in her that they were wrong'? Or perhaps something like, 'A boy from the wrong side of the tracks grows up to help those who had the same start in life as him'? Or, realistically, would it be more like, 'An average Joe from an average town gets married and successfully holds down his average job until retirement?' No judging here – just write down what is true for you.

Then, ask yourself: Are you happy with that sentence you've just written? If you are, great! If not, it's time to head off in a new, exciting direction in life – and it's never too late to do so.

The good thing is, you can rewrite this sentence whenever you want by simply making a decision to do something different with your life. Sounds easy when it's put like that, right?

204.

Here's a basic prompt for you: Eat more fruit today!

We all know fruit is good for us, and the good thing is, it's super tasty too. I'm not saying suddenly become a fruitarian; just add an extra apple and some blueberries to your snacks today, or whatever takes your fancy. If you're not really into fruit or don't like the texture, try making it into a smoothie or a milkshake, mmm!

Personally – if anyone cares – my favourite fruits are: strawberries, pineapples, mangos, blueberries, pears, grapes, apples and bananas. So now you know. Just don't eat too much fruit – although they're full of natural sugar, it's still a type of sugar.

205.

Take a few minutes to watch Lori Harder's TEDx Talk, Turn Your Struggles Into Strengths. It has a great message about stepping outside your comfort zone in order to grow as a person.

There are so many great TED and TEDx talks out there, but Lori's one of my idols and (unknowing) mentors, so I recommend giving this one a go!

206.

Go outside, take off your shoes and socks, close your eyes, and then take several deep breaths, being aware of your feet connecting to the grass, stone, earth, or whatever else you're standing on. Ground yourself and feel connected to nature. You could also put your hands in water or press your hand against the bark of a tree. Just really focus on the textures of the natural elements.

At a pinch – if you don't have an easily accessible outdoor space or if the weather/temperature isn't cooperating – you can still ground yourself if you have a wooden floor, as wood is connected to/comes from nature. There's a whole lot more to grounding, of course, but this is a good start.

207.

Send someone a surprise in the post (and I mean a nice surprise!).

Order them something off the internet or make something yourself and send it to them. You don't have to let them know it's coming, and if you want to be really mysterious, you don't have to admit it's you who sent it (unless them not knowing who sent it is actually driving them mad!). Do it for the joy they'll get out of the gift, not for the credit.

As with all of these things, it doesn't have to be anything huge or expensive. Just put some thought into the gift, getting them something you know they'll like and appreciate.

208.

Brené Brown is everywhere at the moment, and for good reason. She's a prolific author, a wonderful public speaker, and a true thought leader of our generation.

I'd like you to check out her famous TED Talk, The Power of Vulnerability.

I love a good TED Talk, and this one's a great one – check it out!

209.

Grab your notebook and write out your definition of 'strength'. What does it mean to you? What different types of strength are there? Do you feel strong, physically, mentally, or otherwise? In which areas of your life do you wish you felt stronger? What can you do to strengthen certain muscles (whether they be actual muscles or metaphorical muscles)?

Some of us feel strong because we're independent and know how to look after ourselves. For others, strength might pertain to morals and integrity. For some people, it means literally going to the gym and lifting weights – feeling strong physically can also make you feel strong mentally, as if you can take on anything life throws at you. So go on, what does strength mean to you?

210.

Where are you gaining energy throughout the day?

Sit and think about this for a moment (or walk and think about it, if you're feeling energetic). You might gain energy, for instance, when you're exercising. You feel the adrenaline, the endorphins, you might be outside in the fresh air, your body's moving, your mind's working... it's all good. Afterwards, you might feel a little tired, but overall, your body is probably going to feel energised.

You might also feel energised after hanging out with friends and family who make you feel good. You might be full of energy after a meeting or encounter with a colleague or someone you look up to – someone who's on the same level as you and who makes you want to get up and go after your dreams.

Whatever energises you, make a list, and include even little things, such as eating a particular type of food or spending time with a pet.

Then, when you have your list, read it over several times, and ask yourself: How can you include more of these energising activities in your life? Can you spend more time with the people who lift you up (even if it's just a phone call or video call)? Can you exercise more? Can you eat more nutritious, energy-giving foods? Make another list full of ideas and try to weave them into your daily life as much as possible.

211.

Make a list of all the times throughout the day when you're generally losing energy. Obviously, we all get tired sometimes, and we're more likely to have less energy at the end of our day than at the start of it, but I want you to pinpoint any specific times where you know you lose energy due to certain things.

For instance, if you have a bad night's sleep, or if you have a fight with your spouse. Perhaps you lose energy when you're at work and have to attend constant draining meetings. Perhaps you lose energy when hanging out with certain friends or family members, especially if they're constantly moaning about their life or the state of the world or anything and everything else. You probably lose energy after eating a huge meal, or after eating certain things (sugar crash, anyone)? Write it all down and study what you come up with.

Then, when you have your list, read it over several times and ask yourself: how can you stop losing energy in your day-today life? Can you cut out certain foods, or perhaps eat little and often instead of large meals that make you feel lethargic? Can you stop hanging out with the Moaning Michaels of the world (or at least spend less time with them if this is unavoidable)? Can you request that meetings at work be quicker, or come up with ways to make them more efficient? Can you try to communicate more effectively with your spouse and reduce the number of arguments you have? Make a list of all your ideas and try to incorporate them into your daily life.

212.

Get some Elizabeth Gilbert in your life. You might know her as the author of *Eat, Pray, Love*, but she's written so many more wonderful books on all kinds of different subjects.

One of my favourites is *Big Magic*, which delves into the creative process and tells some incredible stories from her own life about how she found – or 'received' – some of her creative ideas. Some of them will surprise you!

Of course, you won't have time to read an entire book today, but perhaps just add this one to your reading list if you're interested in creativity.

213.

You only have so much willpower in a day. Just like energy, it slowly decreases as the day goes on, and by the time the evening comes around, many of us don't have much left at all.

With this in mind, are you making the most of your daily willpower supply? At what times are you spending your 'willpower currency'? Can you perhaps improve on this?

For instance, for many people, doing tasks that require the most willpower first thing in the morning will work in their favour. That's why many people workout first thing, or get the most difficult work tasks of the day done first, while they still have a good stock of willpower.

If you have a work task that requires a lot of energy and brain power, try to do this first thing in the morning – or whenever you're at your most productive. Many of us suffer from the mid-afternoon slump, for instance, so don't try to do the tasks that require the most willpower during that time. Make a list and then rearrange your schedule to see if it makes a difference.

When you spend your willpower, and what times of the day are more effective, will depend on each individual. For instance, some people are morning people, whereas others are night owls. What works for one won't necessarily work for the other. Think about your own energy levels throughout the day and come up with the best times to complete the tasks that require the most willpower.

214.

What is your zone of genius? If you've read *The Big Leap* by Gay Hendricks, you'll know that you generally have four zones: your zone of incompetence, your zone of competence, your zone of excellence, and your zone of genius.

Hopefully not many of us are stuck in our zone of incompetence, but many of us are stuck either in our zone of competence or our zone of excellence. While the latter sounds pretty good, it's the zone of genius we want to strive for, as that's the zone in which we truly thrive, living up to our true purpose in life.

You can find out more about these zones online, so do a little search if you're not sure, but ask yourself: are you stuck in a zone of competence or even excellence? Could you be striving for more? It's time to break through into your zone of genius.

I highly recommend reading *The Big Leap* to find out more about these zones.

215.

Here's a basic prompt for you: Go to bed earlier!

Unless you're already someone who goes to bed early, try bringing your bedtime forward by just five or 10 minutes. You can do this for several days until you're going to bed half an hour earlier, or whatever you want to aim for. Do it in small increments and you're more likely to stick to it.

Sleep is everything, and the effects of sleep deprivation are actually similar to the effects of intoxication, which isn't great news if you're driving on a lack of sleep, or looking after children, or doing anything really.

216.

Think of your life as a book and today as a new page in a brand new chapter – one you're writing yourself. This is the whole premise of the Write Your Life Method, but for today I just want you to take a moment to think about what you want to write in this new chapter.

Forget the previous chapters – they're in the past – and focus on what you want to write now. Surely you want to write something epic and amazing, where you get outside your comfort zone and try something new? Where you take risks? Where you really live life instead of just sailing through it? After all, why would you write a chapter where nothing happens, or one that's so boring you fall asleep reading it? No one would read that, and no one wants that for their life, right?

So, go on, what are you going to write in your next chapter? And think fast, because that chapter's starting today!

217.

Reorganise your work space.

Personally, I can't get to work if I'm surrounded by rubbish and clutter.

Chuck out anything you don't need, or put it away in a drawer, and only have on your desk the things required to do your work. Add some motivational quotes, your vision board, or a photo of your family – whatever gets you motivated – and keep it clean and tidy.

It really is amazing how a bit of cleaning, tidying, and decluttering can change the way you approach your work.

218.

'Get better sleep' prompt: Read in bed until you feel drowsy.

I'd recommend reading a real, physical book rather than anything on an electronic device, as we know blue light is bad for us. I'd also recommend reading fiction last thing before sleep; if you're reading a riveting self-development book where you're trying to really take in all the advice and make mental notes, your brain isn't going to be relaxing any time soon. Remember: sleep is so incredibly important, so anything you can do to minimise distractions and help you get a better night's sleep is well worth doing.

219.

Reorganise your bedroom, particularly your side table or whatever's right next to your bed.

I can't sleep if I'm in a messy, cluttered bedroom, and it just makes it so much easier and nicer waking up in the morning to a clean, tidy room, devoid of crap.

Our bedrooms should be our sanctuary, so get rid of the rubbish!

220.

If the space allows, move around some of the furniture in your living room or dining room – or whatever room you spend a lot of time in.

I moved some things around in my living room – chairs, tables, flowers, plants – and immediately felt better about the space. Sometimes, you just need a change, especially if you spend a lot of time in that particular room and are constantly looking at the same things in the same places. Little changes can make big differences.

And, if you're into it, why not try feng shui-ing the heck out of your room? Where the energy of a room flows from and to could make all the difference – or at least give you a bit of a change.

221.

Sometimes, we focus so much on all the things we haven't yet achieved in life – or all the material things we haven't yet bought – that we forget to look back and reflect on how far we've actually come.

Think back to the 'you' of five years ago, 10 years ago, 20 years ago, and so on. What were you like? Where were you living? What job did you have? What dreams and aspirations?

Were you happy? Did you want to escape your life, or be in different circumstances?

My bet is that the you of the past would be absolutely gobsmacked at where you are now. The job you have, where you're living, your partner, your family, the knowledge and experience and talents you've gained over the years... and just your life in general.

Take a moment to reflect, and journal on it if you wish to. You've come a long way, baby! Don't forget it!

Personally, whenever I'm feeling like I'm not particularly getting anywhere with a project and am feeling frustrated, I think back to the me of 10 years ago. Back then, I would have killed to be self-employed, to be my own boss, and to have the ability to work from anywhere in the world, choosing my own hours and choosing which work I do. That seemed like an absolute pipe dream, and I couldn't actually picture myself doing it (this was before I got into self-development). So, look back at the past you and celebrate how far you've come.

222.

Reframe your mindset around: money.

Do you still think of money as being the root of all evil? Do you believe the phrase 'more money more problems?' Do you think all rich people are annoying idiots? Do you have a mental block around money? If so, you'll probably never earn the amount of money you deserve to. In which case, you need to change your money mindset.

Think of money as simply being energy, a resource that gets passed around from person to person, and exchanged for goods and services. How could that possibly be evil? And there's always enough money to go around; just because you earn a lot of money doesn't mean someone else has to earn less. There is so much money out there, just as there is so much energy constantly flowing around us; you just need to give yourself the permission to take it.

Of course, I mean 'take it' as in 'earn it', not 'steal it', but hopefully you got that. You need to get rid of your money fears and turn them into an abundance mindset. For this I highly recommend the podcast *The Chris Harder Show*, which used to be called *For The Love Of Money*.

223.

There's a famous quote by Joseph Campbell: "The cave you fear to enter holds the treasure you seek."

So, what cave are you currently too scared to enter? Think about it, identify it, and then… enter the damn cave! You never know what treasures you'll get as a reward.

Of course, we're not talking actual caves here, unless you have a desire to get into caving – which, having seen *The Descent*, I certainly have no desire to do. Entering the cave you fear is like opening the door and stepping outside your comfort zone. It's scary, but it's so, so worth it.

224.

If you're a driver, do you ever do a regular drive from point A to point B without really realising you've done it, or without remembering any of the journey? (And no, I'm not talking about alien abduction here!).

When it comes to certain things, we do them over and over again until they become a habit. We don't even have to think about it. Our brain goes on autopilot, and we simply do the thing and get it done.

With this in mind, what else would you like to be on 'autopilot' in your life? What else would you like to have done so many times it becomes a habit? So you don't even have to think about it or deliberate over it – you just do it?

Make a list and see which habit you want to focus on building next.

Exercise can become a habit, healthy eating can become a habit, reading positive books every morning can become a habit, meditation can become a habit... anything can, really, as long as we do it over and over again every day. In many instances, habit is so much more powerful than motivation or inspiration in terms of getting stuff done. So, what do you want to get done today?

225.

One day you'll wake up for the very last time. One day you'll eat your favourite meal for the very last time. One day you'll drink water for the very last time. One day you'll see your friend/family member/partner for the very last time. One day all of this will come to an end.

Make the most of every moment.

Be grateful for everything you have and everything you are fortunate enough to be able to do.

Don't take anything for granted.

Enjoy the little things in life.

Be present.

Be thankful.

I think that says it all.

226.

Reassess a strong belief you've always had, either about yourself, about other people, or about life in general.

If you thought it in the past, do you still think it now? Is this actually your own belief or have you picked it up from somewhere or someone else?

Is it, in fact, the belief of your parents or your grandparents, or the people who came before them? Has it been passed down through generations? Or have you got it from society, from popular culture, from your friends or peers?

Take a moment to really consider whether you actually believe the thing 100%. And, if there's even a tiny chance that you don't, journal on it and find out *why* you don't believe it. Do you have any proof for or against it? Does it actually make sense to you, when you really think about it?

This belief could be anything, such as 'money is the root of all evil' or 'everyone in our family is fat, so you'll never be anything other than fat' or 'people like me, from my kind of background, don't get to be successful in life'. Reassess. Reevaluate. Rewrite.

227.

Some people are glass half full types. Some are glass half empty types. Well, what if you could be another type? After all, whether the glass is half full or half empty, the main thing we all seem to forget is: it's refillable.

Fill up that cup and remind yourself there aren't always just two ways to be; you can always find another outlook in life, another way of seeing things.

Don't be confined to just the obvious methods of thinking. Fill that glass and get drinking!

228.

Find or buy a nice notebook and use it as your 'goal-setting notebook'.

Write out all your goals, then the tasks you're going to complete in order to achieve each goal, and the date you're going to achieve it by (for more info on how to do this, I walk you through it in my *Write Your Life* book). Then, keep a diary of how your tasks are going and how you're working towards your goals and ambitions.

Then, whenever you get frustrated with how little you've accomplished, or annoyed that things are going too slowly, you can flip through your goal-setting notebook and see how far you've come – how many things you've done to get one step closer to your goal, and how much you've learnt in the process. It will keep you motivated to continue, even on your worst days.

229.

'Get better sleep' prompt: Try buying blackout curtains for your bedroom if you don't already have them.

I have them in my bedroom and they're a real game changer, especially if you have streetlights right outside your house. Remember: sleep is so incredibly important, so anything you can do to minimise distractions and help you get a better night's sleep is well worth doing.

230.

Book an eye test! Yes, seriously. If you haven't had one in a while – whether you wear glasses or lenses or not – just book one in and see if there have been any changes.

If you don't wear glasses/lenses and should be, this needs to get sorted, and if your prescription's changed, then it's in your interest to get that sorted too.

Not wearing the right prescription, or not wearing glasses when you need to, can result in headaches, nausea, vertigo, and dizziness – not to mention the obvious: that your vision won't be as crisp and clear as it could be. That doesn't sound fun!

Of course, it's also good to keep a check on your actual eye health, and to make sure there's nothing dodgy going on or looming in the background.

231.

This is one for the ladies: go and get measured for a bra!

Even if you have been measured properly before (and many women haven't), bodies change, so you could still be wearing the wrong size. This can lead to discomfort, pain, poor posture, skin problems, and more. Get the right size and also the right design for you.

For the men – and the ladies, if applicable – check you're wearing the right sized underwear! I know, this sounds ridiculous, but these little things can make a big difference to our daily lives, especially with something we wear every single day. Getting rid of chafing and discomfort means that you can face the day more comfortably, and underwear that is too small can even lead to skin problems and much bigger health issues.

232.

If you're an introvert like me, I highly recommend the wonderful Susan Cain. As an introvert, I loved her book *Quiet: The Power of Introverts In a World That Can't Stop Talking*, as well as her TED Talk, The Power of Introverts. Check them out and be prepared to learn a lot!

Even if you're not an introvert, she has a lot of great insights about the power of being quiet.

233.

This is similar to another prompt in this book, but with a slightly different approach.

Choose someone in your life who you want to get to know better, and ask if they'd be up for a 'Deep Dive Q&A.'

This is when you sit down for a conversation with them (or you can do it over the phone or via video chat) and you ask each other deep, important questions designed to go beyond the usual casual chit-chat and small talk so you can really get to know each other. Here are some example questions:

• What one thing do you really want to do in life that you're worried you'll never do?

• What is your best ever memory?

• What's the worst thing that has ever happened to you?

• What one thing would you change about your life right now if you could?

• What is your biggest regret in life so far?

• Who has taught you the most in life? And what have they taught you?

Pick and choose the questions that most relate to you and the other person, and feel free to come up with your own.

234.

Journal on a current problem you have or a current goal you're working towards – preferably something that's bothered you for a long time, or a goal you've been striving to reach for a long time.

If you're having trouble either solving the problem or actually reaching your goal, ask yourself the following questions: What are you scared of? What are you worried will happen when you solve the problem/reach your goal? And can you trace this back to anything in your past? Think on it, meditate on it, and journal on it – and don't be afraid to dig deep here!

For instance, many people have money issues that go all the way back to their childhood. If their parents quarrelled over finances, they might see money as being a bad thing. A female entrepreneur might be hitting a wall in terms of how much she's able to earn, but why? If she really thinks about it, perhaps she remembers her mum suddenly getting a job that meant she earned more than her dad, and perhaps – whether as a result or not – the girl's parents got divorced. She then grew up thinking she shouldn't earn more than her partner in case it leads to tension and separation. These things from our past matter, whether we realise we're holding onto them or not.

235.

What would you do – today, right now – if you were a character in a book? If you could have your protagonist overcome anything in order to achieve any kind of goal, what would you choose?

This is a super simplified version of the Write Your Life Method, and one that can be done very quickly. What journey would you want your character to go on?

As usual, this exercise will give you an insight into what you want out of life. More adventure? More meaning? More purpose? More fun? More living and less existing? Write it all down!

236.

You are the hero of your own life. Start acting like it.

Sorry to be bossy, but it had to be said!

237.

Pay attention to what you're fuelling yourself with – both your body and your mind.

The food you put in your mouth fuels your body, and we all know that some things are more efficient and more effective at fuelling our bodies than others. Well, it's the same with our minds; we can either fill it with crap – whether from the depressing news we consume to the bitching we see on social media to the friends we surround ourselves with, if they're partial to gossiping or being generally negative and draining – or we can fill it with nice, nutritious thoughts and ideas.

Positive podcasts, self-development books (ahem), peers who lift us up rather than drag us down… it all makes such a difference to your mental health, your attitude, and the way we look at things on a daily basis.

It can help to pause and think before we eat anything, and ask ourselves: Do I really want this? Am I really hungry or just bored? Could I eat something healthier, or that will help my body more? It can also help to pause and think before we consume anything else: books, news, podcasts, TV shows, company… make sure we're fuelling ourselves with the right things.

238.

'Get better sleep' prompt: Wear blue light glasses if using electronic devices in the evening.

These can stop some of the harmful blue light rays from entering your eyes. Of course, it would be better to just stop using devices completely in the hour or so before bed, but this isn't always possible. Remember: sleep is so incredibly important, so anything you can do to minimise distractions and help you get a better night's sleep is well worth doing.

239.

Give positive thinking a go.

I've always believed in positive thinking in a kind of loose, general sense. I always thought that people who think positively are more likely to be happy, are more likely to tackle problems from a more positive place, and will probably have a happier life in general. For me, though, that was it. I didn't delve any deeper, especially not into 'self-help' type books.

But that was years and years ago, and since then, these kinds of books – and websites, and podcasts – have completely transformed. They're full of inspirational stuff, but they're also full of practical things you can do to improve your life, and they're often based on real scientific experiments. A lot of them have ditched the 'self-help' label (I know quite a few people who wouldn't go anywhere near these books simply because of those words) and now use the far more useful – and more accurate – 'self-development' term.

And 'positive thinking' isn't just about thinking positively – it goes so much deeper than that.

As humans, we are constantly learning, constantly growing, and constantly developing. And, if we're not, we should be. When linked with positive words, the power of positive thinking (along with visualisation, affirmations, and hundreds of other tools) can be absolutely incredible.

The things we think about ourselves and our lives matter. Make sure the things you're thinking are positive.

240.

Pay attention to all the words you use today, whether you're talking to yourself, talking to other people, or simply thinking them.

Words are incredibly powerful and they can change the world, but even if words just change *your* world – that's worth everything, isn't it?

Just make sure you use them wisely!

If you realise you're using a lot of negative words – or words with negative connotations – try to cut them out, or at least cut down on them. Also pay attention to the way you're saying certain things – your tone, your volume, everything. We can give words more power by the way we say them, so be mindful of everything coming out of your mouth – and *how* it's coming out of your mouth.

241.

I'm a self-proclaimed introvertpreneur – I'm very quiet and often shy, but I kick ass when it comes to achieving my dreams.

What word – which you can make up, if you wish – best describes you and your personality? This can easily be done by splicing two words together, such as introvert and entrepreneur. That describes both my personality and my job. Can you do the same for yourself?

If so, how would you describe yourself?

242.

"There is gold everywhere. Most people are not trained to see it" – Robert T. Kiyosaki, *Rich Dad Poor Dad*.

I love this quote, and it's so true. How often do we go through life completely oblivious to all the wonderful things and opportunities around us?

So, ask yourself: what 'gold' are you missing in your everyday life? Could there be opportunities out there – for work, for hobbies, for making new friendships and gaining new relationships – that we're just not seeing, either because we're not looking or because we don't believe the gold is actually out there? Write down what you come up with.

If you have a spare 45 minutes, I highly recommend watching episode 4 – The Secret of Luck – of Derren Brown's series, *The Experiments* (available on YouTube), especially the part with the man who is so blind to the opportunities around him that he misses even the most obvious things… until Derren intervenes.

243.

Be aware of what you say repeatedly to other people – especially children and young adults, who are more susceptible to words coming from adults.

I was always a quiet kid – no one's disputing that – but I believe I stayed quiet because of how often people would tell me I was quiet, that I was shy, that there was no point asking 'that one' because she never had anything to say… and teachers can be the absolute WORST for this.

If you were also a quiet kid, you can probably relate to this: did you ever get a report card saying 'she's a good student but she's too quiet', or did a teacher ever tell your parent during parents' evening (or parent teacher night) that 'he's very talented but he needs to put his hand up more'? 'She doesn't speak up enough'. 'He needs to be more assertive in class'. 'She doesn't have the confidence to give her own opinion'.

On the other hand, all the 'loud' kids got great feedback. 'She's very vocal in class'. 'She puts her hand up all the time and has to have an answer to every question'. 'He gives his opinion freely and always has something to say'. They reward the loud kids and scrutinise the quiet kids. And I'm not saying loud kids don't have important things to say; I'm just saying that, in school at least, being quiet is seen as a bad thing, when that's not the case at all.

As I'm sure you know from your own formative years, the things people say to us – especially adults and authority figures – stay with us. They can even shape our personality, moulding who we are as people. So be aware of what you're saying to others; you never know where it could lead – in both negative and positive ways.

244.

Do something new/different today, but do it in your own way – with your own twist.

In the first year of high school our class went on a three-day trip to a 'PGL' centre in Shropshire – a kind of adventure place for schools where you slept in dorms and did all kinds of healthy, wholesome outdoor activities. To 11-year-old me, it was complete and utter hell.

We knew there was going to be a disco on one of the nights so we'd all taken 'disco clothes' with us, but some little twerp stole mine and hid them behind the chimney in the foyer (I found them just before we left to go back home).

Instead of just not going to the disco, though, I turned up in my pyjamas and slippers (the only items of clothing I had left that weren't covered in mud by the end of our stay).

I also hadn't wanted to go kayaking (as we had to do a kayak roll in the water, and I hated going underwater then), so I refused and went orienteering instead, finding my own way.

I was terrified of the zip line, but I did it, and I did it in my own way; instead of screeching all the way down like everyone else did, I remained absolutely silent as I hung on for dear life. The people on the ground thought this was strange, but it didn't matter; I was doing things my own way.

What could you do today, but in your own way?

And it could be anything. Wear something different from the norm, suggest doing something totally different with your group of friends, try a different activity, and so on.

245.

Write down something memorable that happened to you. It can be something funny, something unexpected, or something bad. Writing down bad things that happened to you can be incredibly cathartic, but if you don't feel like you're ready to do that just yet, don't worry. Something light-hearted and fun will be just fine for this exercise.

Write this in the first person, as though you're simply writing in your diary, and really try to remember as many details as you can, as well as how you felt before, during, and after the experience. Let it all out, and if the memory is a painful or bad one, let that pain pour out of the pen and onto the page with every word you write.

Then, rewrite the event in the third person, as though you were writing a scene in a story (you can embellish it slightly to make it more dramatic, funnier, sadder, or whatever works best depending on the situation). Standing on the outside and looking in at the situation should help you see it in a different light and from a totally different perspective.

This can be a really therapeutic exercise, and it's yet more experience of writing about your life in the third person – as if you were an outsider looking in, from a different angle.

246.

Here's a basic prompt for you: Eat more vegetables today!

OK, so most vegetables aren't quite as tasty as their fruity counterparts, but we know they're good for us and a lot of us don't eat enough of them. Just add them to the side of your main meal, or have some as a snack throughout the day – whatever it takes to up your veg intake. You could even drizzle a little butter over them, or some gravy, or whatever else you like to put on them. Just get them eaten.

You don't have to stick to the obvious veg either, such as carrots, broccoli, cauliflower, and so on. Think outside the box and try some vegetables you've never had before, or have ones you only usually have on special occasions, such as Christmas dinner or Sunday lunch. Vegetables are for every day!

247.

Some of us stick with a job because we think it's the sensible thing to do even if we hate it, or we spend every day of our lives in the same towns we were born in because we don't realise there's an entire magical world out there to explore. Or we stay in the same line of work simply because it was the first job we could get when we first started working.

Is there something in your life that you're just 'going along with' because it's always been that way? Even if you don't particularly like it or are bored of it or even actively hate it? Is there something you could do to change this? To shake things up?

Write out one thing you've been going along with in life that you want to change, then come up with a list of ideas as to how you could start making this change.

Things you're 'just going along with' could include: your job/your career/your line of work, where you live, what you do in your spare time, your friendship circle, your hobbies or lack of them, the things you do on a daily basis, your wardrobe/style, your haircut, the make-up you wear or don't wear, how you portray yourself, the music or radio shows you listen to, the TV shows you watch... are any of these boring you, after staying the same for so many years? If so, now's the time to shake things up!

248.

I once had a dream where I was sitting on some bleachers, ready to watch some kind of show in a tent. I knew I was younger, probably in high school – you know, the way you just know things in dreams? – and I was waiting for my friends to join me.

One by one people entered through the gap in the tent, and one by one they walked past, each one choosing to sit far away from me. I didn't know if my friends hadn't come or if they'd just ignored me, but by the time the show was about to start I was still sitting on my own, the bleachers in front, behind, and either side of me completely empty of spectators. How rude!

In the dream, I tried to wrap my head around why this had happened. Was I a loner? A loser with no friends? Was there something so pathetic-looking about me that no one wanted to sit anywhere near me? I thought through each of these things carefully, really rolling them around in my mind, and then the answer came to me: it didn't matter, because I was fine on my own.

I was the cool, independent one who did her own thing, and while I liked having friends, I certainly didn't need them to have a good time. I could have a good time right here on my own, enjoying the show even though no one was sitting next to me.

What's more important was that, in the dream, I didn't care if anyone else thought I was a loner or a loser without any friends. I knew the truth – that I was independent and confident enough to sit on my own without caring what anyone else thought – and that was the main thing.

Have you had any dreams like that? Where something happened, and you knew you could react badly, but you were able to change your mindset to react in a positive way? Try to remember any past dreams you've had like this, and write down the lessons you think your subconscious might have been trying to teach you.

I know that this was only a dream (and a pretty boring one at that) but I woke up feeling pretty damn good about myself, I can tell you. Through that dream, my subconscious was telling me something, and I was more than willing to listen.

Sometimes, we just need to look at things from a different perspective, and often, all we need to do is make a tiny tweak to our mindset. It can take us from a position of weakness, feeling embarrassed at having no friends, to a position of power, wanting to show everyone how independent we are. And that's just one example out of potential millions.

249.

I'm sure many of you have had this fantasy: quitting a job you hate in a highly dramatic and awesome fashion. Of course, (most of us) don't do this in real life as we need references for future jobs, but it's nice to think about, isn't it? Especially if you have (or had) a horrible boss or if you have colleagues who really rub you up the wrong way.

This isn't about being mean; it's about saying exactly what's been on your mind ever since you started your job, and letting people know how you feel.

With this in mind, write a scene in the third person, with you as your character quitting in the way you wish you could (even if you like your current job, I'm sure you'll have had jobs in the past where you fantasised about quitting in such a way).

It can be dramatic and public, like the famous scene in *Bridget Jones's Diary*, or it can be more subtle, where you simply take your boss aside and tell them everything you've ever wanted to tell them. Write a funny resignation letter (the one you wish you could write and actually hand in), or do that thing where you send your team a cake with a passive aggressive message on it. Think how you'd like to quit your job (or a past job) if there were no limitations and no repercussions, and be as creative as you like.

This is meant to be cathartic, and no doubt it will be a lot of fun too. If you're in the enviable position where you love your job/career/business, perhaps write a similar scene where you tell someone in your life exactly what you think of them (if they've been mean to you or put you down, for instance, or if they're constantly trying to put you off achieving your dreams).

If you're happy with your job but want to quit a different situation, such as leaving a relationship that's bad for you, leaving a house you hate so you can move into one you love, or even just phoning up and quitting your internet provider because your internet is rubbish, write about that instead.

Don't be too mean, though; this isn't about turning into a 'Negative Nelly'. It's about standing up for yourself and your dreams – in whatever way you see fit.

250.

Whether you believe in a Higher power or not, do you really think you were put on this earth to work in a crappy job you hate, or live somewhere you don't want to live, or simply plod along, living paycheque to paycheque, just about making ends meet and being constantly stressed about your bank account or what you'd do if you suddenly received an unexpected expense?

To me, the answer is no, that isn't why we're here. It *can't* be why we're here. So, it's time to change anything in our life we're not happy with. Just keep the above question in mind as you decide what you want to change.

251.

Be grateful for the obstacles you've come across in your life – make a list of all the ones you can think of and consider how they've helped you become a better version of yourself (just as failure helps you learn and grow).

As Gabby Bernstein says, obstacles and roadblocks are just detours on your path that help nudge you in the right direction. They help you grow as a person, they help you see what you do and don't want out of life, and they help whittle down the options if you're feeling overwhelmed and confused about which path to take. They can also teach you lessons that you can use in the future, and that you can teach to others.

252.

Whether you're a writer or not, *The Healthy Writer* by Joanna Penn is a really useful book, so have a think about checking it out.

Having suffered from a terrible back injury myself due to working from home and sitting down too much at my desk, I know how important it is to keep yourself healthy when working from home (or if you have a sedentary office job).

So, please read this book and make sure you stay safe and healthy while writing/working!

253.

Our only limitations are the limitations we create for ourselves.

What limitations have you created in your own life? Write them down, then make a list of how you can undo these unhelpful self-imposed limits.

For instance, for years I put all kinds of limits on myself because I believed I was 'too shy' and 'too quiet' and 'too introverted' to even try. Now, I accept that I'm quiet and shy and introverted, and I do the thing anyway. I am capable of doing it if I really put my mind to it – even if I feel huge resistance. The more resistance you feel, the better it will be when you actually achieve the thing you've told yourself you can't do.

254.

Because I'm quiet and softly spoken, people underestimate me. And that is actually a brilliant position to be in, because when people underestimate you and you come out and do something amazing and awesome and awe-inspiring, the impact is far more powerful. When people don't think you're capable of something and you show them that, actually, you are – and not only that, but you're able to really knock it out of the park – it's a pretty great feeling.

Do people underestimate you for whatever reason? Because you didn't finish school or didn't go to uni? Because you're a single mum or dad? Because you haven't gone travelling and seen the world? Because you come across as ditzy or flaky?

Whatever the reason, prove them wrong, and you can start today by writing out your intention to prove them wrong. Read it over to yourself several times, then keep this in mind going forward. You've got this.

This isn't about making someone else look stupid or making them feel bad; it's about showing everyone you're more capable than perhaps even you thought. Make it a positive thing, not a negative thing rooted in revenge.

255.

Take some time out of your day and watch some cute videos online of your favourite animal(s). After all, this is what the internet does best, and as an animal lover, it always puts a smile on my face.

My favourites are videos of dogs, cats, foxes, raccoons, goats, and pretty much any other cute fluffy animal doing anything cute or funny. Sometimes, it's the little things that help us get through the day.

256.

Do you have something coming up that you're dreading? Or that you just really don't want to do? Or something you can't wait to be over? Is there any way you can look at that thing from a different perspective, to help get you through it? Write down some ideas – and for this exercise, the wackier the better.

For instance, I had to go and have an MRI scan of my spine, and I'd heard horror stories of how terrible it was and how it was basically like lying in a coffin. Well, I was determined to look at it from a different perspective – a less coffiny perspective.

Sure, it felt like I was in a coffin, but the loud rhythmic banging sounds weren't unlike some of the music you hear in clubs these days, and in between the thoughts I was having about what work I needed to do on my book and my business, and how I could go about doing certain things (I wanted to use my time wisely), I felt like I was having some kind of one-person rave in a disco coffin.

At times, the bangs and vibrations occurring around me were so loud they rattled my entire body, and I could (almost) imagine I was having a back massage, as if I was in one of those fancy massage chairs.

Suddenly, it didn't seem so bad. I was getting a back massage and I was having a one-person rave in a vibrating disco coffin. Life is pretty funny when you think about it, even if you're doing that thinking while in an MRI machine.

This might seem like a rather silly story, but it's an example of changing the way you think about something and making the most of an uncomfortable situation, and it can be applied to many other areas of your life too. Using my time in a productive way took my mind off where I actually was and why I needed to have the MRI in the first place.

257.

Head out on Fear Highway. That's what I want you to think of every time you choose to do something that scares you, such as trying new things that are way outside your comfort zone.

Picture yourself heading out on Fear Highway in an ultra cool convertible car, the top down, the wind in your hair, the radio blaring some awesomely inspirational rock song, the hot sun hanging overhead as you zoom along the interstate towards a seemingly never-ending horizon.

Then picture your fear, sitting in the back seat. It's still with you – because it's always with you – but it's taking a back seat, and you're the one doing the driving now. You're the one in control.

You're doing something awesome, and you're not letting fear beat you. Enjoy it.

Think of this every time you're about to do something scary, and you'll feel like a badass rather than the trembling wreck you might have been to start with.

I'd recommend choosing an actual track for your Fear Highway theme song to have playing on your car radio, and make it a good one! You can even play it or sing it to yourself before you do the scary thing to bring back this visualisation of you in the car, heading out on the road.

258.

Repetition equals rewards. If you're striving for a goal – such as learning an instrument, starting a new business, getting fit, and so on – find something that works and then do it over and over and over again. Habits equal hope, and repetition equals rewards.

Practice makes perfect. How do you get to Carnegie Hall? Practice, practice, practice!

259.

At the end of the day, write down five things you've accomplished that day, no matter how small or trivial – things you're proud of, things that made you or someone else feel good, things that helped people, things you'd been putting off, and so on.

Then read them through several times and really pat yourself on the back for achieving them. After all, even if they're small, five things a day really add up fast.

260.

'Get better sleep' prompt: Do your daily gratitude practice before bed.

Reminding yourself of all the amazing things in your life and of what you're grateful for can put you in a great mood right before you drift off, and it will hopefully result in nicer, better dreams! Remember: sleep is so incredibly important, so anything you can do to minimise distractions and help you get a better night's sleep is well worth doing.

261.

Commit to giving up one thing (a bad habit, a vice, something you know you shouldn't really be doing) for a month.

If it's something you have to pay for (like booze, cigarettes, takeaways etc.), save any money you would have spent on that thing over the month. Then, at the end of the month, treat yourself to something (and don't just go and buy loads of booze, cigarettes, or takeaways!). Spend the money on a fun experience for you, on a dinner date with your partner, or a day out for the family.

If it's something that was free but that took up time (such as lazing around watching TV, having long lie-ins in bed when you knew you needed to get up and do things, or procrastinating from work), log how much time you think you'd usually spend doing that thing in a month. Then, at the end of the month, use that time to do something positive for yourself that will help get you one (or several) steps towards your goal. Spend it reading a book on the subject or doing internet research, or listening to an informative podcast, or going for a long walk in nature to think about your business idea while also getting some exercise in.

Whatever it is you're giving up, this is also a great exercise in habit-forming. If you can give it up for a month, you can probably give it up for two, and then three, and four, and so on. Well done you!

262.

Today, let go of perfectionism. Let go of the idea of 'perfect'. Perfect doesn't exist, and constantly striving for it isn't going to end well. Think progress not perfection. Done is better than perfect. Scratch perfection from your vocabulary!

I don't mean you shouldn't strive to be great, but if you're putting off finishing something because it's not 'perfect', you're never going to finish. It's just your fear talking, and striving for perfection and never finishing is just another way of procrastinating. Let go of the need to be perfect, in all areas of your life.

263.

If you're looking for a read that's a little out of the ordinary, try *Love On The Rocks With A Twist* by Margaret Anderson. It's a collection of short stories, but each story has 'study notes', in which the author explores the dynamics of the relationship featured in the story, and studies how their decision-making processes either worked or didn't work.

I would have enjoyed this book even if it was just the short stories – which are entertaining and compelling in their own right – but the added study notes really do give this truly unique book that extra something. It made me stop and think about the stories in a different light (and from the perspectives of different characters), and it also made me apply these view points and lessons to the relationships in my own life.

As a big fan of making lists and working through things step by step, I found the author's methods of how to make decisions regarding relationships (and how to come up with a plan depending on the outcome you want) truly insightful.

My favourite stories were 'Duet for Flute and Phantom', 'The Package' & 'Suprise.com'.

264.

Think about when you train a pet, such as a dog. You command them to do the 'move' whatever it is (sit, stand, lie down, paw, roll over, fetch, come back, etc.) and then, as soon as they do it, you give them a treat.

This is a great way of training dogs, but the treat only works as a reinforcement for so long after they've completed the action. If you gave them the treat 10 minutes later, they wouldn't connect the treat to the action they'd completed before. It has to be an instant thing.

Our brains are just the same. When we're trying to form a habit, when we do the thing we want to do, we should either celebrate straight away, or say out loud 'I'm feeling really good right now' – but make sure there's no delay. Your brain will associate this good feeling or this celebration with the thing you just did, and so you'll start feeling that way every time you do the thing (for instance, going to the gym or doing a workout at home).

With this in mind, what can you train your brain to think and your body to feel after a certain task or activity? This will help you form the habit.

And remember to 'treat' yourself every time you complete the task – just make sure it's something nicer than a dog biscuit.

265.

If you're trying a new thing (whether as a result of these prompts or for any other reason) and it's not going so well yet, don't be too harsh on yourself. No one said it was going to be easy, and some things just take time, no matter what.

Think about a toddler, trying to walk for the first time. You wouldn't shout at them every time they fell over, calling them a failure, would you? (Well, hopefully not). You'd just keep encouraging them, knowing that falling over is all part of the process – a necessary part of the process, in fact.

So, make sure to keep encouraging yourself – even if you fall flat on your face – and just give it time. You'll get there. Start today.

266.

Check out my mentor, Lori Harder (www.loriharder.com), who is an awesome fitness expert turned self-development guru. She motivates, inspires, and informs through her online courses, her mastermind events, and her incredible podcast, *Earn Your Happy*.

She does great interviews, insightful 'quickie' episodes, and – my favourite – 'Questionably Awesome', Q&A shows with her friend, Evans, which are so insightful and really funny too. I've mentioned her book, *A Tribe Called Bliss*, already in this book, and I use it to conduct regular meet-ups with my entrepreneur friend, going through each chapter and completing the exercises together.

For today, perhaps pick one of her podcast episodes and give it a go – I'm sure you'll learn something, and you'll most definitely feel inspired, uplifted, and motivated by the end of it.

I've learnt so much from Lori, and I hope you do too!

267.

Don't take advice from someone you wouldn't want to swap places with.

Write this sentence down a few times, then remember it going forward.

268.

If you haven't already seen it, check out *Hamilton: An American Musical*.

Unless you've been living under a rock for the past few years, you've probably heard of this amazing rap musical about one of America's founding fathers, Alexander Hamilton. Written by Lin-Manuel Miranda, this musical fits in with the theme of 'legacy' perfectly (which I talk about a lot), and I highly recommend watching it on Disney+ and/or listening to the soundtrack.

It's pretty long, so if you don't have time to watch it or listen to the whole thing today, just check out some of the songs. My favourite is *My Shot*.

I was fortunate enough to see it live in the West End before the pandemic hit, and I've watched it on Disney+ several times since. You simply have to check it out!

269.

For today I'm going to recommend Oprah's SuperSoul Conversations, which is available on Apple podcasts. Try giving an episode a listen and see what you think.

We don't really get much Oprah over here in the UK, so this is a good place to start – and it's full of fascinating discussions with fascinating people.

270.

As you've probably gathered, I'm all about comfort zones – and stepping outside them in order to go after your goals. So, today I'm recommending *The Discomfort Zone: How To Get What You Want By Living Fearlessly* by Farrah Storr.

There are so many books out there on comfort zones, so if you're interested in this topic, take a look at what's available!

271.

'Get better sleep' prompt: Meditate before bed.

Meditation can help relax the body and mind, so it can help you to switch off, ready for sleep. Mediate last thing, when you're already in your pyjamas and in bed, so that you can simply drift off straight after (hopefully!). Remember: sleep is so incredibly important, so anything you can do to minimise distractions and help you get a better night's sleep is well worth doing.

272.

I've mentioned Chris Harder and his rebranded podcast, The Chris Harder Show. Well, back before he rebranded, he did an awesome podcast episode with an entrepreneur called 'Charlie Rocket' (or Charlie 'The Rocket' Jabaley). I hadn't heard of Charlie before this, but I definitely want to learn more now after hearing his inspiring life story.

The main thing I picked up on, though, was the idea of creating a 'costume'. When Charlie was at school, he decided he wanted to be a businessman, so he started calling himself CEO Charlie and going to school wearing a suit and carrying a briefcase. He created this whole new character – complete with name – and then he became that character.

He did this again, later on in life, when he left the CEO world behind and decided to get fit, lose weight, and start doing epic fitness challenges. Once again, he created a character. This one was called 'Rocket Charlie', and he wore bright workout clothes and bandanas. He was more fun, more casual, but still determined and serious about his goals. With the new name and new clothes (or 'costume'), he became Rocket Charlie just like he'd become CEO Charlie all those years before.

So, for today, check out the Charlie Rocket episode of Chris Harder's podcast (episode 180) and think about the character you want to create.

I promise it will inspire you!

273.

I've worked from home for years, even before the pandemic hit and it became the norm for a lot of people. And, in those years, I've had some horrible things happen to me and my health simply because I didn't look after myself while working from home.

I don't want that to happen to anyone else, so I wrote a blog post: *How To Stay Healthy – Physically and Mentally – When Working From Home* (find it at jessicagracecoleman.com/blog). This applies to anyone who works from home, but it becomes even more important when you're working from home during lockdown – so take a look, and perhaps start implementing some of these ideas in your home office (even if that 'home office' is the kitchen table!).

The tips in the blog post are also useful for people who work in offices, or for anyone who works in the same space for a long amount of time.

274.

For today, I want you to slow down.

That's it. Make sure you take a moment (or several moments) to sit back, relax, and just do nothing for a while. It doesn't have to be 'go go go' all the time – give yourself the time and space you need to rest and recharge.

Life is so hectic, and many of us never take the time to just sit and do nothing – to be at peace, and let our body and mind fully relax, if only for a few minutes.

275.

Today, let's think about fight, flight, or freeze. Can you think of an instant in your past where something happened and you did one of the above? Do you wish you'd done something else?

I can certainly think of one – a rather hilarious one, looking back on it, though it was terrifying at the time – and I talk about it in a blog post I wrote called *What (Not) To Do When You Find A Naked Burglar In Your Room – A Tale of Fight, Flight, or Freeze* (find it at jessicagracecoleman.com/blog). Believe it or not, it's a true account of what happened to me one night on the Thai island of Koh Samui.

Give it a read and then journal on your own fight, flight, or freeze response – and how you could have changed it.

276.

You've probably heard the quote "The harder you work, the luckier you get", or "Inspiration exists, but it has to find you working" (Pablo Picasso).

So, what are you going to work hard on today? What are you going to be working on when inspiration finds you and gives you that spark or that idea you need to complete your goals and achieve your dreams?

In the words of Angelica Schuyler in 'The Schuyler Sisters' from *Hamilton: An American musical*, "Work!" Work it. Get down to work. Get hard at work. Just work. There's no other way through to the other side.

277.

Watch a musical – or a film about songs and songwriting – and see how the characters weave their words, thoughts, and dreams into songs.

It might give you some inspiration for your own goals and dreams, and even if it doesn't, most musicals – the nice, happy, uplifting ones, at least – can be very motivational!

If you don't have time for a full musical, just watch a clip from a musical on YouTube.

278.

Today I suggest you check out the Instagram profile of Jessica Zweig (@jessicazweig). For one thing, she has a great name (not that I'm biased or anything), and for another, she has some great content about personal branding that can apply to people even if you're not building a personal brand.

She also has a great book, *Be*, so if you like her Instagram profile, check it out.

279.

If you were told you had to start a blog on something, what would you write about?

What subject do you already know a lot about, are passionate about, and could come up with lots of content around?

Write down any and every subject you can think of, then look carefully at your list. Is there anything that really sparks excitement in you? Could you actually start that blog? Or start a business around it, or a side-hustle? Or perhaps start a hobby around it, a Facebook group or page, or an Instagram profile?

If you're passionate and knowledgeable about that topic, perhaps you should do something with that passion and knowledge – especially if it helps other people.

Of course, not everyone wants to start a blog or a business, but even just making it into a hobby or starting an online community around it could be a great idea to stir up that passion both in you and in others.

280.

As Steven Pressfield says in *The War of Art*, there's a rule of thumb that "the more important a call or action is to our soul's evolution, the more resistance we will feel toward pursuing it."

So, what are you feeling resistant to at the moment? Is there something you really want to do, but you feel like there's a mental block there? Something stopping you from going ahead with it?

Make a list and then consider each one in turn. Ask yourself:

• Am I feeling resistance to this because I really don't want to do it, or because I really *do* want to do it?

• Am I feeling resistant because I'm scared of what the outcome will be? Scared of failure, or scared of success?

• Is there a chance this thing might be my true calling? Something that will add to my soul's evolution?

Look at your answers and see what they tell you. You'll probably know if the 'thing' is something you should pursue or not.

I felt a lot of resistance when starting my new venture with the Write Your Life Method (especially the 'putting myself out there' bit), but I knew I was feeling this resistance because it was important to my soul's evolution, as Pressfield puts it. I knew I had to get outside my comfort zone and work through the resistance to get to the reward on the other side.

281.

Is there someone you need to forgive in your life? Someone who did you wrong, or betrayed you, or perhaps just did something small that really upset you? Is it time to forgive them?

The key here is that you can forgive the person for what they did even if you still feel upset or angry about it. In fact, in the wise words of Giles from *Buffy the Vampire Slayer*, "To forgive is an act of compassion. It's not done because people deserve it. It's done because they need it."

So, do you have anyone in your life who you need to forgive for something? It can be as simple as deciding to do it, and then doing it. Even if you're not over what they did, it can feel really freeing to finally forgive them.

Obviously this won't apply to everyone, but if you really stop and think about this, you might find there is someone you need to forgive for something – no matter how small that something might be.

282.

This is another book recommendation to add to your collection, and it's one I've already mentioned: *The War Of Art: Break Through The Blocks And Win Your Inner Creative Battles* by Steven Pressfield.

He offers some great insights that come in easy to digest bite-sized pieces of information, so you can dive into the book every so often whenever you have a few minutes to spare. Perfect for those of us who are busy yet hungry for knowledge and inspiration!

As it's short and you can dive in and out, I recommend getting it today and reading a few pages a day over the next week or so.

283.

As the saying goes, you should do one thing every day that scares you, and while I don't necessarily agree with the 'every day' thing, it can be a great exercise to do for, say, a few days at a time.

So, today, I want you to do one thing that scares you.

Before you do anything, though, I want you to write down your ideas for what the 'scary thing' could be, plus a sentence or paragraph explaining WHY that thing scares you. It could be because of a phobia you have, it could be due to the limiting beliefs you carry around with you, or it could, quite simply, be fear – but perhaps not the kind of fear you think.

When you write down why you're scared of doing something, really try to break down that feeling to its smallest component parts. Some might be simple, of course – a fear of skydiving could just be a fear of dying – but some might be a little more complex. The fear you feel around talking to someone new or putting yourself out there, for instance, could actually be broken down to several smaller fears: fear of rejection, fear of looking stupid, fear that it won't go well and that it will put you off ever doing this kind of thing again… the list goes on.

Then, once you've done the scary thing, I want you to write another sentence or paragraph explaining what you did, what the results were, and whether your fears were justified – or whether they were completely unfounded.

If you're finding it difficult to think of scary things to do, don't worry – they don't have to be huge, monumental things like skydiving. Here are a few ideas of things you can easily try this week:

• Talk to someone new

• Make a new friend

• Ask someone out on a date (either a friend date or an actual date)

• Apply for a new job

• Try a new food

• Visit a new place or book a trip somewhere new

• Make that phone call you've been putting off

• If you're an entrepreneur, do a live stream or record a video for social media

• Get that tattoo or piercing you've been thinking about

• Make that decision you've been putting off – sometimes, making the decision is the scariest part

• Join a club or group

Not everything you try will end brilliantly – that's just life – but the more you do the scary thing, the easier it will become. Writing it all down and keeping a record of the scary things you do will help you process your feelings around them, and besides, it's always nice to look back on the things we've achieved.

284.

What would you do if today was your last day on earth?

It's a horrible, terrible, morbid question to try to wrap your head around, I know, but it's also a really good way of getting us thinking about what matters most in life – and what doesn't.

After all, if we knew that today was our last day on earth, we'd probably be doing things a little differently (or a lot differently). We'd ditch the boring stuff, eat the delicious food, and spend time doing what we love with the people we love.

So, why aren't we doing that every day? Why wait until our last day on earth to do the things we love, the things that make us feel good? Why not do what makes us happy right now?

I know, I know. It's not feasible to live every second of every day as if it were our last – for one thing, most people would stop working and the economy would implode within hours – but what if we lived just one day a week as if it were our last, or (at the very least) one day a month? Now we're onto something.

So, grab a notebook or open a fresh document on your computer and write the following question at the top of a brand new page: What would you do if today was your last day on earth?

Without thinking about it too much, I want you to write down the first words, phrases, activities, hobbies, places to visit, people you love, and so on that come to mind.

What do you love doing? Who do you love hanging out with? Where would you want to be? What would you want to see? What would you eat and drink? Would you sit inside and watch TV or get outside in nature and explore? Would you be curled up with a book or would you organise a gathering with friends and family? Perhaps you'd even want to be at work, if what you do helps others and gives you a great feeling of satisfaction. Perhaps you'd go out and give money or time to the people who need it most. Perhaps you'd just sit and be grateful for everything you've been able to do in your life. Perhaps you'd paint or sing or dance or write.

Then, once you have your list, I want you to get a highlighter (either real or on the computer) and highlight all the things you could feasibly do during a normal day or normal week in your life. For instance, you may well be able to go for a walk in nature or visit an old friend, but giving all your money and assets away is probably going to be a big no-no.

Once you've done that, use your highlighted words and phrases to come up with a few sentences or paragraphs visualising what that day would be like. Then, grab your calendar or diary and pick one day in the next week or month when you're going to bring that visualisation to life – and make sure you stick to it!

I'd recommend doing this exercise at least every month, as you probably won't be able to fit everything into just one day and you'll probably keep coming up with new ideas about how you'd spend your 'last day'.

Remember: life is for living and for doing things that bring us joy. So, come on, what makes you truly happy?

If it were me doing the exercise, I know I'd have to write some things down as complete non-negotiables: I'd spend as much of the day as I could outside in nature, I'd make sure I made time to see my family and my closest friends, there would definitely be a lot of tea and chocolate involved, I'd want at least some time alone to sit with my thoughts or read a book somewhere cosy, I'd listen to music and sing along, and I would absolutely have to find some dogs to play with. And, if I could help some people along the way, even better.

285.

Consider this quote from one of my favourite TV shows, *Buffy The Vampire Slayer*:

"The big moments are going to come. You can't help that. It's what you do afterwards that counts. That's when you find out who you are."

We all have the 'big moments' in life, whether good or bad: deaths, marriages, births, the moments you have to step up to the plate, the moments you have to make huge, life-changing decisions, the moments of horror and sorrow.

Write out all the 'big' moments you've had in your life – or, if you've had a lot of them, the main five. Then write a sentence or two about how you reacted to that moment – what you did afterwards. What did it show you about who you really are?

If you aren't immediately sure what it showed you about 'who you are', journal or meditate on it for a while. Did your response show that you'd do anything for your family? That you're willing to sacrifice everything to help someone you love? That you're stronger and more resilient than you thought? Write it all out and be proud of the person you are.

286.

We've had a similar prompt to this one previously in the book, but this one goes into much more detail, so give it a go.

Who you surround yourself with is a big deal. If you constantly hang out with people who do nothing but moan and groan about their life and are always making excuses about why they can't do something, guess what? You're going to find yourself being dragged down to their level, and – as I'm sure you know – it can be exhausting putting all your energy into being so miserable. What's the point?

If, however, you surround yourself with positive, enthusiastic, happy people who lift you up, your energy levels are going to soar – and so will your mood and your mindset. So, who do you surround yourself with on a daily/weekly/monthly basis? And is it perhaps time to rethink the kinds of people you hang out with?

It's time to get really honest with yourself (are you scared yet?). And, while it might seem simple, if you're doing this properly it may well require quite a lot of 'mulling over' time.

So, I want you to get out a notepad and pen and write down the 10 people you spend most of your time with (either physically or virtually). This will probably include your partner if you have one, any immediate family, extended family, friends, colleagues/co-workers, and so on. And, for this exercise, let's leave out the children – after all, if you have kids and live with them, that's not going to be something you can really change (or want to change – hopefully!).

Now, create two columns and title them 'Positive' and 'Negative'. I'm sure you can guess what I want you to do now – split your list into positive people who generally lift you up, and negative people who generally bring you down. Don't try and get five in each – just be honest about where you'd put each person.

I know this can be difficult, as sometimes people can be both positive and negative depending on the situation, but just think about how you generally feel after hanging out with them. Do they bore you, exasperate you, or make you feel bad (about yourself, your life, or anything else)? Or do they make you laugh, encourage you to go after what you want, and leave you feeling energised and happy? Have a think and fill in your positive and negative columns.

For whoever's on your positive list, great! These are the kinds of people you should be surrounding yourself with, and you shouldn't change anything about how you hang out with them (unless, perhaps, it's possible to hang out with them even more). For those on the negative list, however… there's a little more to think about.

I'm not saying you should cut these people out of your life immediately (unless they're really having a negative effect on you, in which case, I'd very much consider doing so); I just want you to think hard about how you let them into your life, and whether this is something you want to change.

So, for each person on your negative list, write a brief paragraph explaining how you feel when you're with them, and how you feel after you've hung out with them – in as much detail as possible. Some people, for instance, might make you feel bad about yourself, your weight, your job, your parenting, and so on, while others might just drain your energy by moaning about their own lives for hours on end.

Once you've written paragraphs for everyone on your negative list, I want you to rate each situation out of 10, 1 being 'I feel terrible after hanging out with this person, and I dread having to see them' and 10 being 'they make me feel a little bad and a little drained, but I can deal with them in small doses'. Compare each person and see who rated lowest. This is the person you need to focus on first.

Finally, I want you to write out several suggestions as to how you could deal with this person, and this will depend on your type of relationship, whether you have to have them in your life or not (family, for instance, can be a tough one), and exactly how you feel when you're with them. Write out all your ideas and then pick the one that will best fit your situation. Here are a few to get you started:

• Cut down on 'physical' time spent with them; instead, talk on the phone or message them.

• Hang out with them only in a group, limiting 1:1 time with them.

• Suggest meeting up for a 'quick' coffee (and give it a time limit) rather than, say, a whole evening of drinking.

• Explain to them how you feel – they might not even realise they're being particularly negative around you.

• Spread out your 'meetings' with them, and make sure you have time to prepare for – and recover from – the interaction.

• Slowly 'phase' them out. If you're the only one who ever suggests meeting up, stop suggesting it and see what happens. If they never take the initiative and contact you themselves, you've got your answer.

- If absolutely necessary, cut them out of your life completely.

Once you've decided what you're going to do, go ahead and do it! Life is short, and surrounding yourself with negative, pessimistic, defeatist people will not only make you feel negative yourself, but it might also stop you from going after your dreams and achieving your goals. So, cut out the negatives, increase time with the positives, and be mindful of how you might be coming across to your own friends and family when you get together – no one likes a Debbie Downer!

287.

Get your notebook and write out the following:

I am grateful for the people I have in my life.

Read it back to yourself – out loud – several times, and then go and message one of those people in your life that you're thankful for.

We often forget the little things we should be grateful for, and writing them down and saying them out loud can help us remember.

288.

It's up to us to write our story, no one else.

Some people wait around for other people to write their story for them – their partner, their family, their friends, their boss, their colleagues, or just the universe, dealing with things as and when they come up and never really planning anything for the future. We are the authors of our own lives, and yet so many people never even pick up the pen.

Well, it's time we did, and one of the ways we can do this is to think of our life as a novel, with us being the main character. This allows us to look at things from a different perspective, and one of the easiest ways to do this is to write our stories in the third person, referring to ourselves as if we were the protagonist of an epic story – where you can't wait to see how it ends. Are you ready?

Some studies have shown that talking about – or to – yourself in the third person can be far more powerful than if you do it in the first person, especially when it comes to self-talk. So why not use this method when you're writing your life? If talking to yourself in the third person can help with self-development, then why can't writing about yourself in the third person help too?

When we talk about ourselves in the third person, something shifts in our brain, so we're going to do this writing exercise not from a first-person autobiographical perspective, but from a third-person fictionalised perspective. This is all about looking at things from different angles, and stepping outside your comfort zone – and writing about yourself in the third person is a quick, simple way to do this.

First, take a few minutes and write a few practice sentences or paragraphs. Write out what you've done today, or what you did yesterday, and then rewrite it from a third-person, past tense perspective. So, 'Yesterday I read a book, went to the gym, and did some work before I crashed in front of the TV' becomes 'Yesterday, Jessica read a book, went to the gym, and did some work before she crashed in front of the TV.'

It's a subtle shift, but a powerful one. You're now looking at your life from an outsider's perspective, and in doing so you'll find you have more self-awareness of what you're doing – and, more importantly, why you're doing it.

Then, I want you to take a particular event from your past – one you remember well – and write it down as if you were writing about the event happening to someone else... say, as if you were writing a scene in a book. Describe the person (you), what they're doing, what they're feeling, what they're thinking, why they're doing what they're doing, and so on, all in third-person past tense. Make it as detailed as possible, and – if you like – add in extra bits here and there to make it more dramatic.

For the last part of this exercise, I want you to write a scene of an event that hasn't happened yet in your life, where your main character (you) achieves one of their biggest goals. Perhaps your character completes a marathon, gets married, graduates from university, launches their own business, moves to a completely different country, goes on an epic trip of a lifetime, writes a book, becomes famous, or kicks ass at a work presentation... whatever it is, write it in third-person past tense, and make it *awesome* – and as detailed as possible.

Congratulations, you've just visualised one of your goals, and writing it down in this way will help convince your brain that not only is it going to happen, but that – when it *does* happen – you'll know exactly how it's going to unfold. Do this for as many dreams and goals as you like, and read back over them regularly – repetition equals rewards!

289.

Have you seen Will Smith's video on failure? (You can find it on YouTube.)

If you haven't, I highly recommend you watch it – it's only short, but it's packed full of amazing advice on failure and, in particular, how we should 'fail early, fail often, fail forward.'

And it's true: a failure is only a failure if we fail to learn anything from it, and fortunately, most failures can teach us a lot – about the situation, about our abilities, and about ourselves in general. The more we fail the more we learn, and the more we learn the more we grow. And guess what? The more we grow, the more successful we'll be.

Failure is good – no, scratch that: failure is necessary.

290.

It's time to slay the day – just like my fictional hero, Buffy the Vampire Slayer. In fact, whenever things get tough or it seems like there's no hope, I just ask myself: What Would Buffy Do?

So, how are you going to slay your day?

For one thing, if it's a weekday and you're sitting there wishing Friday would roll around sooner rather than later – and relying on the idea of the weekend to get you through – stop it!

I've been there, believe me, but wishing your life away is not cool, and it's certainly not going to get us where we want to be. Instead, we need to create a life where we don't wish for the weekends and where we don't wake up every Monday morning moaning and groaning.

So, take out your journal (or hop on your computer) and write/type the following questions:

- What one thing could I do to make today bearable?

- What one thing could I do to make today good?

- What one thing could I do to make today incredible?

- Is there anything I've been putting off because it's too difficult, too time-consuming, or too scary? Could I do that now (or at least some part of it)?

Then, answer each question in as much detail – or with as many different ideas – as possible, and make sure to write it in the present tense as if you're doing these things already.

In terms of the last question, I find that if I've been putting something off for whatever reason and then I decide to simply go and do it that day, the relief and the satisfaction I feel instantly lifts me up, making me feel a whole lot better about myself in general.

If needed, close your eyes for a moment and visualise your day. Would getting an extra treat at lunchtime make it bearable? Would going for a walk on your lunch break while listening to upbeat music make it good, especially when you start releasing those endorphins? What if you phoned up a friend and arranged to meet them later for a meal or a drink? What if you booked that event you've been putting off booking for whatever reason, or enrolled in a webinar or some other form of self-development programme?

Now, you've slayed your day. You're actively working towards achieving your life goals – things that are far bigger and far more important than one single day.

So, instead of holding onto the thought of the weekend to get you through the day, use the day to work towards your dreams, and hold onto *that* thought instead. Because, when you achieve your ultimate goals, it will feel like all your weekends, days off, and holidays have come at once – there's nothing quite like it.

291.

It's time to make fear your friend, and we can start by completing the following exercise.

Write out a few sentences about a time when you felt scared. This could be a time you felt a little bit frightened (like when you had to give a speech or presentation at work, or when you were going for an interview), or a time you felt absolutely terrified (like just before you jumped off a crane for a bungee jump, or if you have a phobia of snakes and one slithered out of the undergrowth directly in front of you).

Explain whatever scenario it is in as much detail as possible: what happened, where you were, what you thought, what you felt, everything. Then I want you to ask yourself the following questions (and write down the answers!):

• Were you scared for a good reason? If so, what was it?

• Did fear help you in any way?

- Could you have mistaken fear for excitement? Could it have been a mix of the two?

- Can you see how fear was just trying to be your best friend?

For instance, if you were going bungee jumping, you were probably scared for good reason: it isn't natural for humans to jump off cranes, even if they're tethered to a rope, and you've probably heard horror stories about bungee jumps going wrong.

Did fear help you? It might have got your adrenaline going, giving you the push you needed to go for it. Could you have been excited as well as scared? Absolutely.

Can you see that fear was just trying to be your best friend? Yes – after all, it was just worried for your welfare, and was trying to stop you from making a potential mistake. In that moment, your fear probably wasn't thinking of the bungee cord tethering you to the crane; it was trying to stop you leaping to your death. It's everything a good friend would be worried about.

This exercise can help you reframe how you think of fear, so go ahead and give it a go.

292.

Athletes use visualisation to improve their performance, and – as various studies have shown – it works. When they can't practise on the court, the field, or the pitch, they're actually able to practise in their minds, visualising themselves becoming faster, beating the other team, winning the race, or whatever it might be.

And, in terms of results, it's almost as good as practising in real life. Pretty cool, right?

What's even cooler is that we can take this idea and use it in our own lives, practising for when we finally get to achieve all our wildest dreams.

So, how does visualisation work?

In layman's terms, when we complete an action – such as reaching out and picking something up – the same part of our brain is activated as when we simply visualise doing that action. In effect, our brain can't tell the difference. It's the same if we visualise ourselves giving a presentation, or crossing the finish line of a marathon, or getting that promotion or award at work.

When it comes to visualisation, no detail is too small to imagine, and the more time you spend imagining whichever scenario you're visualising, the more your brain will think you're actually doing it, and the easier it will be for you to actually achieve it.

Repetition equals rewards, and the more you visualise something (with exactly the same thing happening each time), the more your brain remembers that pattern and the easier you'll find it when you actually come to do it; your brain will think it's no biggie (real science talk there) as you'll have already 'done' it several if not hundreds of times before.

If we can then take those visualisations, write them down, and read them back to ourselves every so often, even better. And that's where this exercise comes in.

As with meditation, visualisation should be done when you're alone, unlikely to get interrupted (so put your phone on silent!), and when you're either sitting or lying down in a comfortable position. Take a deep breath, close your eyes, and start visualising the thing, right from the start.

When you're finished, take a few moments to breathe deeply before opening your eyes again, and give yourself a few more seconds to adjust back to the present. Then – and this is the important bit – I want you to write down that visualisation in as much detail as possible, and do it in the first person and in the present tense, as if you are actually doing the thing as you write/type it.

Write down what you're doing, who's there and how they're reacting, what you're thinking, what you're feeling, what you can see, and any other little detail you want to include. But, most importantly, make sure you write down exactly how you're feeling as you achieve that goal – how proud you are of yourself, how happy you are, how relieved, how fired up, how inspired, and how completely and utterly amazing you feel. Then read back over it, again and again.

So, whenever you're feeling stuck in your pursuit of your goal, get out your notebook or open that Word document and read through your visualisation (even adding more details to it, if necessary). This will remind you what you're aiming for, as well as giving your brain more ammunition to go after this goal and achieve it for real – which is exactly what you're going to do, right?

293.

For today's exercise, I want you to write either a poem or a song, and it doesn't matter how short or how long it is – as long as you write it from the heart and as long as it relates to your life (or even just your week. This is a thing you can do every week to make sense of the past seven days).

This, of course, can still be an incredibly hard thing to do, so let's start small – with a haiku. If you're unfamiliar, a haiku is a type of short poem originating in Japan that has a very specific structure: three lines, with five syllables in the first line, seven in the second, and five in the third line. Often, haikus are deep and profound, but you can write them about anything you like.

Here's an example I just came up with:

Write Your Year with me,

It could even change your life...

If you do the work.

Not very poetic, I know, but hopefully you can see the structure now.

Why not try writing a haiku at the start or end of every week, perhaps with one idea or one thing you learnt from the week that's just gone by, or perhaps concerning the main issue or problem you've had to face in the last seven days? Hey, you could even write them all down in one notebook or Word doc, and in several months you'll have your very own haiku collection! That's pretty cool, and it can be very therapeutic too. Give it a go – what have you got to lose?

294.

Another book recommendation today, though it's a little different to the usual self-development books I recommend. The book is *The Magic Seeker* by Marla Martenson, and I loved it.

This book gave me some wonderful and much-needed escapism, which is important in life, but it also gave me great insight and wisdom. I found Marla's life so full and fascinating, and as someone who is interested in spiritualism but who hasn't had too much direct experience with it, I found the book both intriguing and educational.

There are also more human elements to the book, which look at how relationships work for different people, from Marla's clients and friends to her own relationship with her husband. Why not give it a try, even if you think it's not your 'thing'?

There are so many nuggets of wisdom in this book, and the fact that they're woven into a highly entertaining read makes it a lot easier to take them in and think about them in relation to your own life.

295.

Today, I want you to pen a letter to your younger self. It could be to your five-year-old self, your 10-year-old self, your 16-year-old self, your 21-year-old self... or perhaps pick more than one. This is similar to another prompt in this book, but we're going to tackle it from a different angle.

In your letter, you can include the following:

- Describe what you're doing in the year 2021 (or whenever you're reading this): Where you live, who you live with, what you do for work, what you do for fun, what strange hobby you picked up in lockdown, and so on.

- Any advice you wish to give to your younger self, either generally or with regards to a specific situation. You can include any words of wisdom you've been given over the years, or bung in some motivational/inspirational quotes you think might help.

- Any achievements you're proud of. This can be anything: writing a book, raising a family, raising money for charity, starting a business, running a marathon, visiting lots of different countries, landing your dream job, earning that promotion, getting married, earning a certain amount of money, winning an award… anything you've achieved over the years that required hard work and determination.

- All the things you love (or have grown to love) about yourself and your life in general.

Then, once your letter is finished, imagine being that five-year-old, or that 10-year-old, or that 18-year-old (or whatever age you chose), and imagine that you're reading this letter from your future self.

Would your past self be surprised at what you're doing with your life? Would they be impressed with your achievements? Would they feel reassured by your advice and words of wisdom? Would it make their life easier knowing they're going to achieve so many awesome things in the future, even if it might seem hard for them to picture it at that moment?

Sometimes, all it takes is looking at things from a different perspective – or a different age!

Remember, all the past events in your life and everything you've ever been through have led you right here, to this place in the present, and have moulded who you are as a person. Are you happy with the person you've become? Are you content with where you are right now? Or at least excited about the future and what you're going to do with it?

Really think about this for a moment before you write down what you'd say to your past self – and be honest with yourself. If you're not happy with who you are and where you are at the moment, perhaps you do have some advice to give to your past self. If you are happy, perhaps you just want to tell them it's all going to work out fine. What you tell your younger self should really tell you everything you need to know about your current situation, even if you've never admitted it to anyone (least of all yourself) before.

296.

Write a letter to your fear (yep, this is gonna be a weird one!) about a recent scary incident you've had.

Address it 'Dear Fear', and then write your fear a heartfelt 'thank you', explaining what happened during your scary incident and why you're grateful for fear's input. Write as if you were talking to a real person, and think of fear as being a friend who was just trying to help you out. For instance, you might write:

Dear Fear,

Thank you for your input when that snake slithered onto my path during my walk in the forest the other day. You made me leap into the air and screech like a little girl, which was embarrassing –

especially as that family of four happened to see me do it – but I understand that you were just trying to help. You were simply alerting me to the danger, even though this is England and the chances of me dying from a snakebite are very low (and I'm not talking about the alcoholic drink).

Still, I appreciate it, and your intervention made me keep more of an eye out as I finished my walk – which is never a bad thing. You also got my heart rate up and caused me to run away from the snake, which must have burned a few more calories, so when I got home I treated myself to a cake to make up for it. I guess I've got you to thank for that as well.

Best wishes,

Jess.

Make it as funny as you want – after all, life is funny, and sometimes we just need to laugh at ourselves and the things we're afraid of. Go on, give it a go (no matter how silly it seems)! Then, whenever you come across a scary situation in the future, or whenever you feel THE FEAR threatening to overwhelm you, just remember that it's trying to be your friend – and be grateful for it. You can even complete this exercise again to remind you of that fact.

297.

Comfort zones – we all have them. You might even be in yours right now, sitting down in a cosy chair with a nice cup of tea, all safe and warm while the chaos of the world swirls around outside.

It's a nice place to be, for sure, but if you have big goals in life, staying in this cosy space isn't going to help you achieve them. We can only grow and develop (in any area of life) by leaving our comfort zone and trying new things.

It can be scary, but if you think of your comfort zone as a comfy room that you can always go back to after trying the new scary thing, it doesn't seem too bad. You don't have to open that door and step out into the swirling chaos forever – you can pop in and out as and when you want to, and every time you do pop out of your comfort zone, your world is going to become a bit bigger (and far more exciting).

So, how can we put this into a writing exercise?

First of all, I want you to write a paragraph or two describing what your 'comfort zone' is like for you. Describe it as if it were an actual place – perhaps a room in your house or somewhere outside – and add in a few details here and there so you can really picture it in your mind.

I'm sure you've heard the expression 'happy place' – as in 'close your eyes and go to your happy place' – and if you've ever pictured this, it's probably similar to your comfort zone. You might be on a beach, or in the middle of a forest, or high up in the mountains – or you might be in a cosy reading nook, reading your favourite book while the rain falls against the window. Picture it in your mind, then write it down.

Next, write a description of how you're going to get out of your comfort zone, however you want to imagine that – just make sure you make it something fun and exciting. For instance, if you're in a room, you could open the door and walk down a brightly lit corridor full of other doors – colourful doors with signs such as 'possibility' and 'growth' on them, which open to new and exciting places you couldn't even imagine from the cosiness of your comfort zone.

Or, if you're nestled in a cosy cabin in the mountains, you could get dressed up in your winter gear and venture out into the snow – and perhaps take an epic zip line down into the valley. Anything that gets you excited or raises your adrenaline.

Make your 'comfort zone exit strategy' as creative or as random as you like, but make sure you can picture it clearly – and then write it down. Read over both passages several times until they're fixed in your mind (and, if needed, come back to them on a regular basis).

Now, every time you go to do something outside your comfort zone, you know exactly what you need to do: picture yourself leaving that cosy room, or that sunny beach, or that beautiful view from high up in the mountains, and heading towards the thing you need – or want – to do.

If you've made your 'comfort zone exit strategy' into something fun and exciting, you'll (hopefully) feel that sense of excitement every time you leave your comfort zone in the real world, and hopefully this excitement will override any fear you might have about the new thing you're trying out.

And just remember: after you've done the scary thing, you're allowed to retreat back to your nice, cosy comfort zone, put your feet up, and relax, safe in the knowledge that you've achieved something amazing – and grown that little bit more. Now you can recuperate for a while before venturing out again.

298.

If you haven't already done so, give yoga a go today. After all, it has so many benefits for both the body and the mind.

There are loads of videos online for beginners, so pick one and see where it takes you.

Who knows? Maybe it will inspire you to find a local yoga class or to find someone who can teach you one-on-one.

If you're not into yoga, try pilates or something else – choose something you enjoy as you'll be more likely to stick with it.

299.

For the next week (either first thing in the morning or at lunchtime – basically, the same time every day so you won't forget to do it), list one thing you're thankful for and why – but make it so the thing you're thankful for starts with the same letter that the current day starts with. If you have to connect it with a certain letter, it makes you think a little harder. So, over the next week, my daily gratitude list might look like this:

M – I am thankful for money! Yes, you're allowed 'material' things. After all, without money I wouldn't have my house, electricity, water, food, clothes… all the things that make daily life manageable.

T – Toilet roll. I don't know about you, but I'm thankful there's not a toilet roll shortage at the moment like there was during the first lockdown of the COVID-19 pandemic!

W – Women! In particular, powerful businesswomen I can look up to – and there are a lot of them out there.

T – Tea. I love tea – in this sense, I'm a super stereotypical Brit.

F – Fries. Who doesn't love fries?!

S – Stories. I love reading, and I've read a lot this year.

S – Self-employment. It can be hard – really hard – but I love the freedom and flexibility it gives me, something that came in especially handy during the pandemic.

There we have it. It's simple, easy, and it gives you a little boost every day of the week.

300.

Is there something or someone you're tolerating in your life? Perhaps something that's been lingering around for years, that you just put up with simply because it's been so long that it's never even occurred to you to do anything about it?

Well, it's time to stop tolerating. Life's too short to tolerate. If it's not helping you in any way, if there's no purpose to it, and if it's becoming a burden, put a stop to it.

We tolerate all sorts of things in our daily lives, and sometimes we don't even notice we're doing it. We sit with gritted teeth during a catch-up with someone we've realised we don't actually like anymore, we put up with someone's bad behaviour because they've always been that way, or we allow people to walk all over us because we've never stood up for ourselves before. Well, it stops now. Stop tolerating things and people that are no longer serving you.

301.

Make sure you're getting your vitamins.

If you're eating a healthy, balanced diet, you probably are, but if you know – for instance – that you don't eat as many fruit, vegetables, and leafy greens as you perhaps should, then you might be deficient in certain vitamins.

Taking something like a daily multivitamin supplement can help, but ask in your local health food shop for advice if you're not sure. (And be aware that many generic multivitamins won't do what you need them to do).

A lot of this depends on your diet. For instance, as I'm a vegetarian, I need to make sure I'm getting enough iron in my diet. There's a lot of information online regarding this, so take the time to do some research if you feel like you're not getting all the vitamins your body needs.

302.

Forgive yourself, for whatever you need to forgive yourself for.

Forgive yourself for not completing things in the past, for not following through with things, for giving up on things.

Forgive yourself for not being as strong or as independent or as intelligent or as brave as you think you should be.

Forgive yourself for putting yourself first or for prioritising certain things over others.

Forgive yourself, for whatever you need to forgive yourself for. It's OK.

Stop beating yourself up and forgive yourself. Now you can move on.

I've talked about forgiving other people. Now it's time to forgive yourself.

303.

Today, I want you to really listen to your body (and I don't just mean if your stomach's growling or gurgling).

This means paying attention to how certain things and people make you feel, and how your body reacts to them.

Does your body react in certain ways when you see specific people? Do you get butterflies fluttering in your stomach when you start working on your new venture? Does your body tighten or contract when you think of doing something you don't want to do, or can you feel your body relaxing and expanding when something feels in alignment for you?

Our body gives us so many signals throughout the day, but we often just ignore them. Today, pay close attention and see what you learn.

These could be obvious things like your stomach churning or a tightening feeling in your chest, or less obvious signs like your breathing changing slightly or feeling a slight tingle run up your spine. Pay attention to the signs and figure out what they mean – they could really help you in the future.

304.

The whole idea of my Write Your Life Method is to stop simply floating through life, reacting to whatever comes your way, and actually write out what you want your life to be.

It's about designing your dream life and going after your goals.

This, however, can seem a little daunting to some people, so for today's writing exercise I'm going to tell you how you can simply Write The Next Day Of Your Life.

In my book, *Write Your Life*, I ask you to imagine that your life is a novel, and that it's up to you to write your next chapter. For now, though, I'm going to ask you to imagine that your life is a movie script – something that is far shorter, and that we can take one scene at a time, no matter how small that scene might be.

So, get out your notebook or Word doc and write out your 'scene' for the next day. Just take one important aspect of your day and write it in advance, including any important dialogue, stage directions, and descriptions of what's happening in the scene. If, for example, you have a presentation at work tomorrow, write out a scene where you're articulate, witty, and informative, and where you absolutely smash that presentation.

If you're planning on asking someone out, write out the scene where you do just that – maybe make it a little flirty, or funny, or whatever you're going for (and, obviously, in the scene you're writing, the other person will say yes!).

If you need to have a tough conversation with your boss, a colleague, your partner, or your child, write out that scene, including exactly what you're going to say and how you're going to say it. Think of it as a dress rehearsal, or a visualisation done in a slightly different way.

You can then read through your scene several times, imagining what it would look like if it actually were a movie scene up on the big screen.

Then, when tomorrow rolls around, you'll be far more prepared for what you need to do. Besides, thinking of your life as being a movie or a novel is always entertaining. Who knows? Maybe you'll win an Oscar… or a Golden Raspberry Award.

305.

Get your notebook and write out the following:

I am grateful for my health.

Then, read it back to yourself – out loud – several times. Even if we have health issues, most people reading this are healthy enough that they can function on a daily basis and go after their goals, and not everyone has that luxury.

We often forget the little things we should be grateful for, and writing them down and saying them out loud can help us remember.

306.

Trust yourself. Completely. Implicitly. Blindly, even.

I'm sure there's been a time when you've gone against your gut instinct and regretted it, or not listened to what your body or your mind was trying to tell you about a certain person or situation. If we'd only trust ourselves, we might be able to avoid some of the bad circumstances we find ourselves in.

So, take out your notepad and write down the following words, several times, before reading them out loud, several times. And really mean it:

I trust myself completely. I trust that I know what is best for me and I trust that I know instinctively what to do in order to go after my dreams. I trust that I can do whatever I set my mind to. I trust that I will keep myself safe and protect myself and my loved ones while I do so. I trust that I've got this. I trust myself completely.

You might think that you trust yourself, but do you really? We can always learn to trust ourselves – our instincts, our gut reactions – more, so give it a go and see what happens.

307.

Many of us kept diaries when we were younger – I know I did. What we did at school, who our best friends were, who we fancied… I mean, what else was there to write about back then? And some of us continue with this tradition as we get older. I did for a while, on and off, but writing a diary just takes so much time, doesn't it?

These days – now that I'm a huge advocate of writing everything down, from what you did today and how you felt about it, to what you're grateful for, to what your goals are for the next week, the next month, the next year... – I tend to spend a lot of time writing things down. It helps me to clear my mind, make sense of the things going on in my life, and even make huge life-changing decisions.

But what if you simply don't have the time to keep a regular diary or journal? Well, that's what today's writing exercise is for!

What if I told you that you could keep a DAILY diary and still have time to fit in all the other stuff that inevitably ends up filling our days? Well, it's true – you can – and the secret? Diary entries don't have to be long. They don't have to be epic tales that fill pages and pages. They can be one page. They can be one paragraph. They can be one *sentence*. That's right – I'm challenging you to keep a one-sentence diary going for the next week or month – or year, if you really want to commit to it.

It is exactly what it sounds like. Every evening I want you to get your diary and write an entry in one sentence. It can either be a summary of what happened to you that day, the main feelings you encountered that day, or just one thing that stood out for you from that day. Then, when you look back at it, you'll get a snapshot of your past few days, weeks, or months, and you might start to see patterns in what you did and how that affected your mood or mindset.

For instance, my past week might look like this:

Monday – I got everything on my to-do list done and felt super accomplished.

Tuesday – I didn't get many 'productive' things done but I felt that my brain needed the rest.

Wednesday – I felt refreshed after my slower day on Tuesday and got right back to it!

Thursday – I had a takeaway burger and chips and felt rubbish (even though it was tasty).

Friday – I had a long Zoom chat with my friends and felt uplifted and relaxed.

Saturday – My lie-in made everything better.

Sunday – Day of exercise and then early night – now I can face the next week ahead!

Then, when you can summarise your day in just one sentence, you can start applying this practice to other parts of your life too. What else have you been putting off because you 'don't have the time' or because 'it will take too long'? What other activity can you condense into a much shorter version but still have it be useful?

Just take HIIT training, for example. Instead of going for an hour-long walk on the treadmill to get your exercise in, try high-intensity interval training, which uses short bursts of intense exercise to get your heart pumping (with periods of rest in between). Suddenly, your exercise for the day goes down from an hour to, perhaps, 10 minutes. So, what else can you shorten or condense in your daily routine? It might be easier than you think.

308.

Whenever I know I need to do something but don't really feel like doing it, or whenever I find myself at risk of going on an all-expenses paid trip to Procrastination Land, I ask myself a question: Will this help or hinder my future self?

For instance, if I'm constantly putting things off and moving things from today's calendar to tomorrow's, I know I'm making things harder for my future self, giving her more things to do that, realistically, I could get done today.

It works the other way around too. If I have a day where I'm feeling energetic and full of beans, I'll look ahead in my calendar and do things off my future to-do list, as I know I'll be helping out my future self, leaving her with more time to either relax or get on with other stuff.

Just take the idea of getting fit and healthy. I know that going for a walk today will help my future self get fitter. I know that sitting on the sofa and eating an entire pizza will not help my future self in the health stakes.

For today's writing exercise, therefore, I want you to visualise your future self – whether it's your future self next week, next month, next year, or in 10 years' time – and ask yourself, what can you do today that will help them out? What can you do tomorrow to help them out? What can you do next week or next month? And, as with everything we do, I want you to write down your ideas. Describe what you can do to help your future self, and then – this is the important bit – write down a sentence or two explaining why this is so important, both to you now and to your future self. Here's a quick example:

Today, one thing I can do that will help my future self is: exercise for 30 minutes. This will give present me a sense of accomplishment (plus some much-needed endorphins) and it will help my future self continue to be fit and healthy, which will give me the energy I require to achieve all my goals.

Next week, one thing I can do that will help my future self is: sign up to that business course I've had my eye on for months. For present me, this will be something to celebrate, as I get to tick something off my to-do list (which I love doing). This will also be invaluable for future me as I will learn practical business tips, it will give me ideas for future ventures, and it will help me grow, both as a businesswoman and a person in general. By enrolling in something I have to pay for, I'll be putting some 'skin in the game' and will be more likely to stick with it until completion, making the most of the lessons it provides me with. My future self will love everything I learn – as well as the fact that I finally got around to signing up!

You get the idea. Once you've done this, put the tasks you've come up with in your calendar or diary, and keep yourself accountable! Your future self will thank you for it.

309.

Check out the blog post I wrote about the pandemic: *How The Pandemic Allowed Me To Turn My Life Around – And How You Can Do It Too* (find it at jessicagracecoleman.com/blog).

In it, I look back and list the ways I got through the pandemic and all the various lockdowns. Hint: it has nothing to do with Netflix.

It's all about remaining positive, productive, and as healthy as possible while you look to the future and decide what you really want out of life.

It also explains how and why I came up with the Write Your Life Method.

310.

For today's writing exercise, I want to take you back to the Halloweens of your youth (assuming you dressed up for Halloween. If not, just pretend you did!) – or, perhaps, the Halloweens of the past few years. Can you remember any of your costumes?

Over the years I've been a witch, a pirate, a pirate wench, a flapper girl, a witch again, a pirate again… clearly, I need to up my Halloween game. Anyway, I want you to write down a costume you remember wearing, and then write down the answers to the following questions in as much detail as possible:

• Did you feel different to your normal self when wearing this costume?

• Did you walk differently, or move differently in general?

• Did you speak differently? Did you give yourself an accent or use words you normally wouldn't use?

• Did wearing the costume make you act in a different way than you normally would? For instance, did you feel more confident? More attractive (or less attractive, depending on the costume)? How about more outgoing?

• Were you more likely to do things outside your comfort zone, or outside what you'd usually do?

• Did you feel a bit deflated when you had to take the costume off and go back to your 'normal' self?

Now, I want you to imagine that you're going to wake up tomorrow and become any character you want to be.

Who would you be? What name would you give yourself? What clothes would you wear? What accessories? How would you speak and move? What goals would you have? Would you be more confident, more outgoing, more willing to put yourself out there no matter what the consequences might be?

Whatever it is, write it down in as much detail as possible. Then, once you've finished, you'll have your very own 'character profile', and guess what? If you want to, you CAN wake up tomorrow and become that character (or at least start to, by adding things to your wardrobe and changing the way you act, bit by bit) because, let's face it, who's going to stop us?

We can be whoever we want to be – just like at Halloween – because what is life if not an opportunity to constantly reinvent ourselves? All it takes is some guts (and maybe a shopping trip for some new wardrobe items).

So, who are you going to be? CEO Samantha? Fitness fanatic Fred? Book-lover Bob? Healthy Hannah? Author Andy? The sky's the limit!

311.

Give yourself permission. Ah, but permission to do what? I hear you ask. Well, it could be anything, but basically, give yourself the permission to go after what you really want.

It might be the case that you already know what you really want in life – have known for a while, perhaps – but that you've stopped yourself from going after it for a multitude of reasons.

Because you have responsibilities. Because you don't have the time. Because there are other, more important things to be doing and sorting out. Because it's not all about you. Because other people rely on you. Because you can't justify spending that much time or money or effort on yourself. Because because because.

It's time to stop with those 'becauses'. This is me giving you permission to give *yourself* permission. Go after your dreams. Do what you really want in life. And do it for yourself. You deserve it.

Be warned: once you give yourself permission to go after what you want in one area of your life, you'll be more likely to do it in other areas too, and before you know it, it'll be a permission fest. This stuff is addictive!

312.

Watch Robert Waldinger's TEDx Talk, What Makes A Good Life? Write down notes as you watch and then journal on them afterwards.

Do you agree with what he says? Are you surprised by what he says? What do you think makes a good life?

Spend some time really thinking about this, and write down what you come up with.

313.

Today I'm recommending another book: *Happy* by Derren Brown. I read this book years ago, and seeing that he has another book out, *A Little Happier*, I think I might need to give it another read before I get the new one.

I love Derren Brown – from his TV shows to his paintings to his books – so will pretty much buy anything he puts out there, but this book really does get you thinking about the nature of happiness. Why not give it a try?

314.

First off, I want you to write down 10 things you've failed at in your life – and these can be big or little things. Here are some examples (some from my own life, some not):

- Dropping out of university or school
- Quitting a course
- Failing an exam
- Not passing your driving test on the first go
- Starting a project and failing to finish it/see it through
- Backing out of something, perhaps out of fear
- Attempting something new only to get rejected or laughed at
- Asking someone out and them turning you down

- Losing a race

- Coming last in a competition

I'm sure you can think of loads, but just pick 10 for now.

Next, pick the top three (or perhaps it's the bottom three) failures – the ones that really make you squirm when you remember them, or that make you feel embarrassed, humiliated, or just plain terrified when you picture them in your mind.

Then I want you to write a sentence (or a few) explaining exactly what happened, and – most importantly – how you felt about what happened. You can either write this like a diary or as if you were writing about a fictional character in a novel, referring to yourself in the third person (this works well if you want to try to distance yourself from the cringeworthy memory). This exercise can be particularly cathartic just on its own, especially if you've been blocking out these memories for years.

Once you've done this, take each failure in turn and write out what you learnt from it – no matter how big or small (or silly) the lesson. Here are a few examples of things (not mine!) you might write:

- In dropping out of university, I discovered that the subject I thought I wanted to study actually wasn't for me at all – saving me a lot of time and money in the long run.

- I failed to complete the marathon I was training for, but in doing so I realised I'm not a cardio person – now I've joined the local gym and am lifting weights instead.

- I've tried and failed to start many different businesses, and although none of them stuck, I learnt skills from each and every experience – admin skills, bookkeeping skills, market research – as well as gaining contacts in the business world.

- I failed to keep my relationship from falling apart, but I learnt so much that I can now take with me into my next relationship: how to communicate, how to give each other space, how to listen, etc.

- When failing my driving test, I learnt not to drive through a hedge into a field of sheep (this actually happened to someone I knew! But don't worry – the sheep were OK).

Can you see how many lessons you've learnt over the years? And can you also see how you took those lessons and applied them to other situations you came across afterwards? It can be a real eye-opener to see them all written down, especially with the ones where the lesson is harder to see.

Once you've done this exercise for all your past failures, you can keep it going as and when you fail in the future (and you *will* fail in the future, but remember – that's not a bad thing!). Every time something goes wrong or you feel like a failure, do the above exercise, and be as detailed as you can in your answers. It can make you feel a whole lot better about your situation, and the more you do it, the easier it will be for you to change your perspective and the way you look at things.

So, if you come across an obstacle on the way to achieving your dream – or if something you try well and truly fails – don't despair, and certainly don't let it stop you. Analyse the failure or the obstacle, understand what happened and why, and then learn from it, taking those lessons with you into the future.

315.

Create – or at least plan out – a vision board!

I know, I know, some people think vision boards are ridiculous. They think they belong to 13-year-old girls who are planning their dream dates and writing in their dream journals. Well, that might be the case, but vision boards are also great tools for adults who want to plan their future goals and dream big.

If you make one and put it in a place you'll see every day (next to your bed, or your desk in your home office, for instance), not only will it inspire you to keep working towards your dreams, but it will also get your mind used to seeing the things you want to achieve on a daily basis. And the more you see these images, the easier it will be for you to go out there and achieve your goals.

I've got my own vision board next to my standing desk in my office, and I look at it whenever I'm feeling stuck, uninspired, or unmotivated. It's like a visual accountability buddy, keeping me on track in terms of my goals and ambitions.

First, I want you to take out a notepad and write down everything you could possibly want to include on your vision board. For instance, some categories might include:

- Your career goals

- Your health goals

- Your home/house goals

- Your travel goals

- Your Legacy Vision and your Success Sentence (These are taken from my book, *Write Your Life: The Ultimate Life Hack For Achieving Your Dreams*)

- Motivational quotes

- Anything else you can think of!

Once you have your list of everything you want to include on your vision board, the next thing you need to do is figure out what you're using for your vision board and where you're going to put it. Are you going to have a physical pin board on your wall? A page or two in a scrapbook? A virtual one, like with Pinterest?

Next, find all the photos you need online. Print them out, cut them out, and then apply them to your vision board (if you're doing a physical one). I highly recommend listening to upbeat, uplifting music while doing this, or perhaps a motivational podcast or two. This is a fun exercise, after all, so have fun!

And that's it – you should now have a nice, pretty, colourful vision board that is positively bursting with inspiration and motivation. Look at it daily. Hourly, if you want. It works.

316.

As American actor Will Rogers said, "Don't Let Yesterday Take Up Too Much Of Today."

Which things, events, words, actions, or experiences from yesterday are you letting take up your precious time today?

Let them go and just look forward.

317.

I've suggested writing a letter to your past self, and now I'm going to suggest the opposite. What would you write in a letter to your future self? Bearing in mind that we probably won't remember all the little things (that feel like HUGE things right now) that are bothering us in 10, five, or even one year's time.

This can be a useful exercise to do, especially if you actually write the letter, put it away (somewhere safe!) and then come back to it in a few months or years. It might seem like a long time, but it can be a great lesson to learn: that the things we're obsessing over now aren't as important as we think, and that we probably won't even remember them in several years or even months. Of course, some problems ARE huge and rightly so (pandemic, anyone?), but we'll just be focusing on the little things in our letters.

So, with this in mind, it's time to write our letter to our future self. In the letter I want you to explain what's happening, what your days have been like recently, and any little problems or concerns you've been having lately. Here's an example of what you might put:

Dear Future Jess,

Today has sucked. It's cold and grey and it's been constantly raining, and we're in lockdown so I haven't been out much. The most excitement I get is popping into Aldi, though I try to be quick because wearing a mask is a bit annoying, and if I spend too long there I'll end up buying a whole trolley load of cheese and probably a toolkit and a dog bed and lots of other random stuff I don't need, purely for the 'thrill' (not many thrills going around these days).

The neighbours are loud and annoying, there's nothing much on the TV, and everything just feels a bit rubbish. I keep wanting to order in food but I know I shouldn't, and I can never decide between pizza, curry, and a big burger. Or maybe twenty doughnuts.

The power went out before, and I got SO annoyed that I couldn't get on the internet for an hour – it's like living in the Stone Age. Oh, and Asda were out of Biscuit Brew; they gave me normal tea bags in my food delivery, and they weren't even Yorkshire Tea ones!

It's meant to rain for the next week, not that it's really that surprising in England, but still... why is everything so crap?

Kind regards,

Past (Annoyed) Jess.

Even 10 seconds after writing that I can see how ridiculous it is, and if I were to write it on an actual piece of paper and put it in a drawer, coming back to it in several months' time, I'd probably just laugh at it. Certain issues might be annoying at the time, but in the grand scheme of things, they're really not worth worrying over.

318.

Take a food sensitivity test.

Even if you don't think you have issues with any foods (or beverages), doing a food sensitivity test can be interesting.

And don't worry – you don't have to draw blood or physically go somewhere and pee in a cup. The one I did (www.simplyhealthchecks.com) just required me to send in several strands of hair, which I took off my hairbrush. Totally painless.

Of course, don't rely solely on the results of these tests, as the results can sometimes depend on other things (such as any food you had in your system when you took the test, and so on). Still, it's a good indicator of any foods or food groups you might have issues with, in which case you can either gradually reduce them in your diet or try an elimination diet, which the website talks you through.

Please note that food sensitivities are not the same as food allergies. For the latter I'd recommend seeing a doctor, especially if you're having really bad reactions to certain foods.

319.

Beat impostor syndrome at its own game.

Let's talk about impostor syndrome. I suffer from impostor syndrome all the time, and I'd say that most people I know who have their own businesses do too.

One day you can feel completely in control of your life and confident in your skills and the value you're providing for others, and the next you feel as if you don't know anything whatsoever and wonder why people would even consider paying you for your services.

You fear being 'found out' by all your clients, or you worry that your work won't be good enough and that all your customers will suddenly turn on you, demanding their money back and bad-mouthing you all over the internet.

These fears are real. They're also completely ridiculous, and (usually) unfounded. But how do we convince ourselves of this fact?

If you find yourself experiencing impostor syndrome on a regular basis, here's a quick exercise you can do to help get you through it.

Basically, whenever you start to feel like a fraud, get out a notebook and write down all the reasons why you're *not* a fraud – and give as many examples as possible.

For instance, because I'm not part of a big corporation and because I haven't been running my business for 30+ years, impostor syndrome often rears its ugly head when I'm running my writing and editing business. So, to remind myself that I'm good at this and that I'm not a fraud, I might write out the following:

• I've been running this business for almost seven years, and it hasn't failed yet.

• I have many repeat customers, and they wouldn't keep coming back if I was doing bad work.

• I get quite a bit of work due to existing clients recommending me and my colleagues to their friends, so we must be doing something right.

• I've been able to make a full-time living from this business.

• I know I hit my deadlines and provide good customer service.

• There will always be a small minority of people who won't be happy with the work, and that's OK. Writing is subjective, and if they don't like the style or the direction I've taken something, it doesn't mean I'm bad at what I do. Not everyone has the same tastes.

• I get good feedback and glowing testimonials from the vast majority of my clients.

Writing out what you're doing right – instead of obsessing over the things you might be doing wrong – can help you overcome impostor syndrome and can also encourage you to believe in yourself enough to follow your dreams. This works for your job, your career, your personal life, your family life, and so on.

Just remember: no one is born with a manual for life. No one really knows what they're doing, and that's OK. You're not an impostor, you're not a fraud, and you absolutely deserve any and all success that comes your way.

320.

Give the book *Worthy Human: Because You Are the Problem and the Solution* by Tracy Litt a go.

It's a great book full of wisdom, and Tracy Litt is like a breath of fresh air – especially when she's encouraging you to dance and get your body (and mind) moving in her online videos!

Check her out and get yourself moving in the right direction.

321.

"The bad news is time flies. The good news is you're the pilot" – Michael Altshuler.

So, what plane are you flying today? Where is your destination? Who (if anyone) is on board with you? Do you have a co-pilot that you trust?

Just like how you're the author of your own life, you're also the pilot of your own plane, and you can fly it wherever you want.

So, where do you want to fly today?

OK, I'll stop with the plane analogy now, I promise.

322.

If you wake up in the morning and think you're going to have a rubbish day, then you probably will. If you go into something with nothing but negativity and fear of what could happen or what could go wrong, then you won't get very far – and even if you do, the outcome probably won't be all that great. Basically, if you think something's going to suck, it probably will.

So make sure you keep positive thoughts in your mind today, and if you find yourself having a negative one, nip it in the bud. Stop it in its tracks, and replace it with something positive.

What's one positive sentence you could think (on repeat) today to change things around? Try these:

- I've got this.
- I can handle anything.
- I'm so lucky to be able to do the things I do every day.
- I have everything I need right here.
- I am bursting with potential.

- I can achieve anything.

Say these positive sentences to yourself whenever you start to feel negative, or just generally throughout the day.

323.

Learn something new today.

We're currently living in one of the most exciting times to be a learner.

You know what? I'm going to repeat that: *We're currently living in one of the most exciting times to be a learner.*

We have more options than ever before when it comes to learning all kinds of things. There is so much technology available – so many apps and websites and pieces of software right at our fingertips – and it's never been easier or more fun to enrol in a course, find a mentor, do research, or watch informative videos.

You should be making the most of this technology, and of the instant connections you can make with other people online. If you have a computer or smartphone and access to the internet, the world really is your oyster. It's a very, *very* exciting time to be a learner, so get excited and get learning!

What thing – or things – are you going to learn today?

324.

Today, remind yourself how awesome you are.

Whenever we feel down, useless, or stuck in a rut, it can be difficult to remember all the great things we've already achieved in life – things that show us the potential we have to accomplish really cool and interesting goals.

Instead, we focus on the negatives: the dead-end job we hate, the house that's crumbling down around us, the salary we thought would be a lot bigger by now, the fact we haven't gone on a decent holiday in years, and so on and so on. Well, it's time to stop focusing on the negatives and start remembering the positives.

I want you to get your journal or open a Word document and write down every single 'success' you can think of that you've already had in life. Basically, anything that you feel proud of, anything that you saw to completion, and anything that you accomplished despite having a load of obstacles thrown in your way... it all counts as being successful.

Did you earn a degree at university? Have you bought a house? Given birth and/or raised a child? Started your own business? Overcome one of your biggest fears? Run a marathon for charity? Rescued an animal? Landed your dream job? Won a competition? Been interviewed for a newspaper or magazine? Helped someone out when they really needed it?

All of these are successes, and they all need to be remembered, but – most importantly – they need to be written down! Just thinking about them isn't going to cut it. So, I want you to write them down and look at them regularly to remind yourself just how freaking awesome you actually are.

Then, once you've written down as many as you can think of, whittle them down to your Top Ten Successes.

You can do this in several ways: go by how you feel when you remember the achievement, go by how many people your accomplishment impacted, how much it changed your life, how fun it was, or how difficult it was to achieve. Your top ten doesn't have to consist of earth-shattering, life-changing events; if they meant something to you, that's all that matters.

At this stage I'd also recommend writing a little paragraph or two about your accomplishment, reminding yourself why you did it, what you had to overcome in order to do it, and why you're proud of it. This can be a real eye-opener of an exercise, as you might remember things you'd forgotten, or you might start thinking of things from years ago in a different light. Give yourself some time to complete this exercise; you might need quite a while to remember all your past successes and, besides, it's fun!

325.

I've got another website and podcast recommendation for you today: Being Boss, a community for entrepreneurs, business owners, and creatives. I love their wonderful podcast, so give it a go today while you're getting ready, cooking, cleaning, exercising, or doing any other activity where you can listen to a podcast at the same time.

I listen to podcasts throughout the day; I pop them on my phone and then carry it around the house with me while I get ready and do my daily chores.

326.

Today, we're going to do some worldbuilding.

Writers do this when they're creating a whole new world for their fictional stories, especially if that world is different to the 'normal' world – if it's set in the future, or in space, or in a parallel dimension, and so on. They delve into the geography of the place, the history, the politics, the people, the specific locations, the language, the clothes, the types of jobs... everything you can think of to build a 'real', believable world – even if the setting is remarkably *un*believable compared to our world. They might write this out, gather photos and maps from the net, visualise it... all the stuff.

So, why am I rambling on about worldbuilding? Well, because it's something we can do for ourselves, in our own little parts of the world.

If you could, what world would you create for yourself? Where would you live? Who would your friends be? What job would you have? What would you spend your days doing? What would you do in your spare time? What world would you build up around you? Write it all out and, if you like, scour the internet for suitable photos and/or drawings, just like writers do when they're worldbuilding.

If you hadn't already guessed, the answers we come up with for this exercise will tell us a lot about what we really want out of life (within reason – unless you created a sci-fi world just because it was 'cool'!). With this in mind, is there anything you can do to make your everyday reality more like the world you just created in your head (or on paper)? Even just one little thing? Think it over for the rest of the day.

327.

Today, I just want you to be OK with not being perfect. We've mentioned perfectionism before, and how to think of progress not perfection, but this time I want you to consider 'perfect' in relation to yourself.

No one and nothing is perfect, so stop striving to be everything for everyone all the time. It's OK to not be perfect. In fact, we're all perfectly imperfect, and that's fine. That's great.

When we stop trying to be perfect all the time, it gives us the time, strength, and energy to do other things – such as working towards our goals.

328.

Time is money. Time is energy. Time is currency. So where are you spending your time today?

Some of the time you spend will, of course, be non-negotiable. You have to go to your job, you have to look after a child, you have to drive your children or spouse somewhere, you have to cook, and so on.

Some of the time you spend today, though, will be up for grabs – even if you think it isn't.

For instance, if you have to commute, could you use that time to read a book on a subject you want to learn more about? Or listen to a podcast that will inspire you and motivate you to go after your dreams? You could also listen to a podcast when cooking, cleaning, or doing any other chore.

Could you spend 10 minutes (or 20, or 30) less a day mindlessly scrolling through your phone and, instead, put that time to better use?

Our time is finite and it is precious. Make sure you're making the most of yours.

If you think of time as being actual currency, it can be easier to decide where you want to 'spend' it.

329.

Have you ever tried EFT? This stands for Emotional Freedom Technique, or you might have heard of another term for it, 'tapping'.

It's an alternative treatment you can do on yourself, and it involves tapping on certain pressure points on your face and body, usually while saying certain sentences specific to you and your situation. It is used to reduce anxiety, stress, depression, and loads of other things.

Even if you're not into this kind of thing, it's worth looking into, and there are loads of videos online that teach you how to do it. The best thing is, it doesn't take long to do. So, why not give it a go today?

Check out Marie Forleo's What Is Tapping video with Nick Ortner (available on YouTube) for an introduction to EFT.

330.

It's human nature to expect the worst, especially when we're trying something new for the first time or something that's way outside our comfort zones.

"What's the worst that could happen?" was a question asked in many Dr Pepper adverts, and of course, it always ended with the absolute worst thing happening – usually to hilarious effect. Of course, it wouldn't be so funny if it happened to us in real life.

Well, if at any point today you find yourself worrying about the 'worst outcome' of something you're about to do, stop, pause, and rethink. Instead, ask yourself:

• What's the best thing that could happen?

• What's the most exciting thing that could happen?

• What's the most unexpectedly wonderful thing that could happen?

It's a mindset switch, and the more we do it, the more we train ourselves to expect the best and not the worst. And, if we're always expecting the best, we'll just go ahead and do the thing. We won't second-guess ourselves or our actions, we won't go into it feeling afraid, and we won't stop ourselves from even trying.

Expect the good out of life, and you'll start seeing it everywhere.

331.

Get your notebook and write out the following:

I am grateful for my body.

Then, read it back to yourself – out loud – several times. Many of us don't like certain things about our bodies, but just pause for a moment and consider how truly amazing our bodies are. They are truly remarkable.

We often forget the little things we should be grateful for, and writing them down and saying them out loud can help us remember.

332.

It's another TED Talk time! Check out Adam Grant's TED Talk, The Surprising Habits of Original Thinkers.

Make some notes as you watch it and then write down your own thoughts around the subject. Have you learnt anything new?

Just be careful – once I watch one TED Talk I inevitably watch another, and another and another, until I've fallen down a massive TED-shaped hole. It's great for learning, but not so great for getting other things done!

333.

"What you get by achieving your goals is not as important as what you become by achieving your goals."

This quote is attributed to a couple of people (Henry David Thoreau, Zig Ziglar), but what's important is the message, because it's one I truly believe in.

Every action we take, every experience we have, every tough time we make it through, every piece of knowledge we take in, every lesson we learn, everything we achieve… it all moulds who we are as people. Sometimes these things change us in little ways, sometimes they change us in huge, monumental ways, but every single one of them transforms us somehow.

So, what sort of person do you want to become? And are your current goals going to get you there?

If they're not, perhaps it's time to rethink those goals.

334.

You can make your own wake-up call.

Don't wait for something huge or dramatic or awful to happen to give you a wake-up call and prompt you into action. Take action right now on what you most want to do in life.

Many people don't leave jobs they hate or move countries or start their own business – or whatever their dream is – until they have a huge wake-up call, such as a health scare or a financial issue. Don't wait for the wake-up call. Make one yourself and spring into action today!

335.

Get your notebook and write out the following:

I am grateful for my sight/hearing/taste/any other sense you want to write.

Then, read it back to yourself – out loud – several times, and really feel thankful for the senses you have. Many of us take them for granted.

We often forget the little things we should be grateful for, and writing them down and saying them out loud can help us remember.

336.

American football coach Vince Lombardi said, "It's not whether you get knocked down, it's whether you get up."

Life will knock us down – it's inevitable – but as long as we get back up, that's all that matters. It's how we react to the things that happen to us that will change our future, not necessarily the actual things that happened to us.

So, can you think of a time when you got knocked down and then immediately got back up again? (Either figuratively or literally!). Write it all down, in great detail, then consider how awesome you were for getting straight back up. Many people wouldn't have been able to.

And now I have 'Tubthumping' by Chumbawamba in my head: *I get knocked down, but I get up again, you're never gonna keep me down...*

337.

"Whether you think you can or think you can't, you're right."
– Henry Ford.

This is a really famous quote, and it's famous for a reason: it's true.

So, I want you to write down a list of all the things you think you can't do or have thought you couldn't do in the past, such as:

- I can't do maths.
- I can't run.
- I can't spell.
- I can't dance.
- I can't earn more than I'm earning now.

These could be to do with work, family, travel, how much money you earn… anything. Then, change those sentences to simple 'I can' sentences, and repeat them to yourself – out loud – 10 times. Start training your brain to ignore what you've told yourself in the past and to reframe what you're able to do going forward.

This quote can apply to so many things in your life, so it's worth taking a moment to ponder Ford's wise words.

338.

Here's another podcast recommendation for you: Happier with Gretchen Ruben.

If you want to get happier, give it a go!

I could recommend podcasts all day long. I listen to them every day and I've learnt so much from them it's insane. Without podcasts, I wouldn't have started my new venture or created the Write Your Life Method. So give it a go and get inspired!

339.

What baggage are you carrying around with you?

We all have it, though some baggage is heavier than others. Some might be a huge case we check in and then don't see for a while, while other baggage will be smaller hand luggage we carry with us everywhere.

So, what are you carrying?

For this exercise you can either write a list or – to have a bit more fun with it – draw a picture. Draw yourself (a stick figure will do, if you can't draw – like me) carrying a piece of luggage, and in that luggage draw all the things you carry around with you on a daily basis – or at least representations of those things. Perhaps you could draw the suitcase half open, with all the stuff tumbling out, or perhaps just draw the case and have the things as stickers on the outside of the suitcase. Whatever you find easiest.

Baggage might include limiting beliefs, past quarrels you've been holding onto, grudges, failed relationships, bad experiences, even physical material items, such as the old car you've had for ages that keeps breaking down and stresses you out on a daily basis. Write it all down or draw it all out.

Then, once you've done it, consider your baggage for a moment and then screw up the piece of paper and throw it in the bin.

I know, it's not that easy to get rid of baggage we've been carrying around with us for years, but it's a good start – and it can feel great.

340.

Reframe your mindset around: past crappy jobs.

If you've had as many crappy jobs as I've had – and by crappy I mean boring, mundane, rubbish pay, horrible bosses, annoying colleagues, stressful, not what you want to be doing, and so on – you'll know that it's difficult to look back on them with anything but irritation, and perhaps even hatred. But the good news is we can reframe them, putting them in a far better light.

Every job I've ever had has taught me something. I've either gained knowledge from it, gained experience I could put to use in the future, gained a reference, or it's taught me what I *don't* want to be doing in life, which is incredibly important.

Even my three-day run as a temp in a call centre taught me some valuable insights: that I didn't want to work in a call centre, and that I didn't want any job that involved me having to get up at 4 a.m. every morning. Screw that.

So, what have your past jobs taught you? What did you gain from them? Take one of your past jobs and make a list of every good thing that came out of it. It might have been a stepping stone to another job. You might have met your bestie in the office there, who you still hang out with today. You might have realised which tasks you love doing and which tasks you hate doing. Perhaps you had a kind of mentor there, who helped teach you something. Whatever it is, write it all down and reframe how you look at that crappy job!

341.

Is there an elephant in the room?

And no, I'm not talking about an actual physical animal – I'm talking about the old saying, where there's something really obvious hanging in the air but no one wants to talk about it.

The type of elephant depends on the type of room you're in. There will be different elephants in the room where you hang out with your friends compared to the elephants in the room you share with your partner, and so on.

So, is there an elephant in the room you're in right now? If you're at home with your family, consider if there's one there. If you're out at a friend's house, consider if there's one there, and so on.

If there is, give the elephant a break and just bring up the subject already! Life's too short, and we don't want our precious mental space being taken up by hundreds of elephants, do we?!

Visualising this can help. Elephants are big, and I don't want them taking up all the space and air in the rooms I'm in!

Bring up the subject – open the door and let that poor elephant out!

342.

Get your notebook and write out the following:

I am grateful for the clean air I get to breathe.

Then, read it back to yourself – out loud – several times, while taking several deep breaths.

We often forget the little things we should be grateful for, and writing them down and saying them out loud can help us remember.

343.

Albert Einstein said, "Life is like riding a bicycle. To keep your balance, you must keep moving."

Do you agree with this? Write down the quote and then journal or meditate on it for a while. How does this apply to your own life?

Personally, I think it's a great quote. Every day, we need to do something – even if it's a small something – to keep moving the needle, to get us one step closer to our goals. So what are you going to do today to keep moving?

344.

Do you often find yourself needing external validation for certain things in your life? We all do it.

We want likes on our posts, comments from our followers or online friends, compliments, encouragement, proof that what we're doing is good and that it matters.

Well, what if you didn't need that external validation? What if you validated yourself just fine?

I want you to write out all the things that you find you often need external validation for. Your appearance, your job performance, your ability as a mother or father, your skills and talents, your feelings and ideas, and so on. Then, cross each one out and write next to it: 'I validate myself. I don't need anyone else to validate me or to validate my feelings/ideas/appearance', whatever it might be. Then say it out loud several times to really drive the point home.

This exercise can cover all different areas of life, as – even if we don't admit it – many of us are constantly seeking validation. We just need to learn to get it from ourselves.

345.

Get your notebook and write out the following:

I am grateful for the fact that I get to eat today.

Read it back to yourself – out loud – several times, and then go and really enjoy the next meal or snack you're going to have.

We often forget the little things we should be grateful for, and writing them down and saying them out loud can help us remember.

346.

If you're feeling stressed or anxious, listen to a podcast aimed at reducing these feelings, such as The Calmer You Podcast.

You could also try A Mindful Moment, The Daily Meditation Podcast, or Social Anxiety Solutions.

347.

Stop future tripping.

Future tripping sounds like it should be something cool – possibly involving a DeLorean and a crazy, white-haired professor – but it's actually not that great. It's a problem many of us have, even if we don't realise we're doing it a lot of the time. Simply put, it's worrying and obsessing over the future, instead of enjoying the present moment.

Future tripping is also called anticipatory anxiety, and I'm sure a lot of you can relate. We constantly worry about the future (especially during, say, a pandemic), catastrophising everything in our lives and expecting things to go badly.

We start a new relationship and spend most of our time expecting something to go wrong. We worry about starting a new job or changing careers, instead of feeling excited about the new opportunity. We let our anxiety run our present, instead of focusing on how amazing our present actually is. It can majorly suck.

But we CAN turn it around. We don't have to spend our time future tripping, and the first step – as with a lot of things in life – is simply becoming aware of when we're doing it. Once we can start identifying our future tripping habits, we can tell ourselves to stop. Not easy, I know, but the more we do it, the easier it will become.

Worrying is just praying for things we don't want, and I'm sure we could put the time we spend worrying to better use – like working towards our goals.

So, today, if you find yourself – at any point – worrying about something that hasn't happened yet, or planning for the worst possible outcome of something, or just generally feeling anxious about what the future holds, stop it!

Every time you realise you're doing this, take a deep breath, close your eyes, and tell yourself – firmly but lovingly – "Stop future tripping."

It's so easy to start future tripping without even realising it, which is why it's important to become aware of when we're doing it and to tell ourselves to stop.

348.

Get your notebook and write out the following:

I am grateful for being alive.

Then, read it back to yourself – out loud – several times, and consider just how lucky you are to be alive right now.

We often forget the little things we should be grateful for, and writing them down and saying them out loud can help us remember.

349.

If you're on Instagram, check out @angieleeshow.

She's a podcaster, marketing wiz and all-round awesome female entrepreneur, and the videos she posts are both informative and hilarious.

And even if you're not on Instagram, you can still take a look at her profile!

350.

If you didn't know, TED Talks are also on podcasts – and there are several TED podcasts to choose from. Find them all at www.ted.com/podcasts and give one a go today.

If you just want to listen to the TED Talks in audio form, try TED Talks Daily.

351.

Get your notebook and write out the following:

I am grateful for clean drinking water.

Read it back to yourself – out loud – several times, and then go and drink a nice, cool, clean glass of water. So many people in the world don't have access to this most basic human right, so enjoy and be grateful for every last drop.

We often forget the little things we should be grateful for, and writing them down and saying them out loud can help us remember.

352.

I love this quote about goals: "Goals are dreams with deadlines" (sometimes attributed to Diana Scharf Hunt).

This is so true. We can have wild dreams about how we want our futures to look, but we're never going to get there unless we take those dreams, pull them down from the sky or the ether or wherever they're floating about, and turn them into tangible goals with specific, actionable tasks and realistic deadlines. That's what my *Write Your Life* book is all about.

So, what dreams are you going to turn into goals? Pick one and give it a deadline, right now, in your calendar.

353.

Today, why not read my blog post, *When Was The Last Time You Had A Movie Moment?* at jessicagracecoleman.com/blog?

I talk a lot about movie moments as part of my Flip The Script Travel Transformation Services, and this blog post will give you a brief introduction to the topic.

Then, ask yourself: when was the last time YOU had a movie moment?

354.

Get your notebook and write out the following:

I am grateful for the goals I have and the dreams I'm working towards.

Read it back to yourself – out loud – several times, and then go and do one thing to help yourself move towards one of your goals. Many people don't have any goals or dreams – they're simply focusing on surviving – so it's a real luxury we don't often address.

We often forget the little things we should be grateful for, and writing them down and saying them out loud can help us remember.

355.

Answer the following question with the first thing that pops into your head. Ready? Go!

What do you most want out of life?

…So, what instinctive answer did you come out with? Did it surprise you or was it something you already knew?

Write down what your immediate response was, then think about it for a few minutes – really think about your answer to the question. If, in those minutes, you come up with a different response, write that down as well, then compare your two answers.

How do your two answers (if you have two) differ? Which one seems right to you? Or can you combine them together to come up with one ultimate, awesome uber-answer?

356.

Ask your friends, family, partner, colleagues, or anyone else you trust to list your three best qualities.

You might be surprised at what they come up with, and you might start seeing yourself in a whole new light – the way your loved ones already see you.

This is assuming, of course, that the qualities they list are positive; if they list negative things, it might be time to reconsider their position in your life!

This can feel a little weird – and you might feel awkward asking – but the more you ask, the easier it becomes. Just tell them it's for an exercise from a book (which it is). Generally, people are willing to help.

357.

If you're in the mood to listen to amazing women who are kicking ass in business and in life in general, listen to an episode of Lindsey Schwartz's Powerhouse Women podcast.

I found Lindsey Schwartz through Lori Harder's Earn Your Happy podcast, as they both do a joint event together.

358.

Get your notebook and write out the following:

I am grateful for the fact that I'm able to read these words right now.

Read it back to yourself – out loud – several times, and then go and read something else that is useful, informative, or inspirational. Having the ability to read is something a lot of us take for granted, especially as it opens so many doors for us throughout our lives.

We often forget the little things we should be grateful for, and writing them down and saying them out loud can help us remember.

359.

Andrew Carnegie said, "If you want to be happy, set a goal that commands your thoughts, liberates your energy and inspires your hopes."

So, what commands your thoughts, liberates your energy, and inspires your hopes? Write down every single little thing you can thing of, either in a list or a mind map (or one big doodle, if you like).

Write it all down and give it all a good ponder!

360.

Reframe your mindset around: success.

We're all striving for success, but are we striving for someone else's version of success? Success doesn't have to mean earning so much a year or being number one in your field, so stop putting so much pressure on yourself.

Yes, I'm all about achieving your dreams, as long as they're your own dreams and not someone else's. This is why I get people to come up with their 'Success Sentence' – what success means to them – after which it's up to you to change your mindset when it comes to success.

You can still be happy when your friends get that promotion or when that influencer you follow online reaches seven figures in their business, but just remind yourself that their version of success is not necessarily *your* version of success, and we don't all have to want and strive for the same things in life.

361.

Get your notebook and write out the following:

I am grateful for the technology I use on a daily basis.

Then, read it back to yourself – out loud – several times, and think of this sentence every time you use a piece of technology today. Where would we be without it?

I certainly wouldn't own an online business, or have quite so many contacts all over the world!

We often forget the little things we should be grateful for, and writing them down and saying them out loud can help us remember.

362.

According to American author Zig Ziglar, "A goal properly set is halfway reached."

Do you agree with this?

I do. So many people don't have any goals in life – not above making it through the day, or perhaps eventually getting a better job that they enjoy more than their current one, or maybe some day getting married and having kids. Those are pretty vague and generic.

If you have even one goal that is specific and written down on paper, you're miles ahead of so many others. As Zig says, you're halfway there.

So, make sure all your goals are written down on a piece of paper and make sure you put it in a place you see daily!

363.

Do a quick review of the last 12 months. What have you achieved? What specific tasks or activities did you complete? What goals did you tick off your list? How has your life improved?

We often forget to look back and really feel proud for all the things we've achieved – even the little things – so now is the time to do it, no matter where you are in the year. This isn't just something that should be done on December 31st before the new year starts; you can do it at any time, looking back on any time period.

Write out all the things you've achieved – I bet it's more than you expected – and then take a moment to really think about each one. Feel grateful that you were able to achieve whatever it was. Feel proud of yourself. Remind yourself that, when you put your mind to it, you can do awesome things. You can do *anything*.

And then celebrate!

364.

If you've done what I suggested at the start of the book and bookmarked the prompts you found the most interesting, most fun, and most useful (and the ones that had the biggest impact on your daily life), it should now be easy for you to go back through all your favourite ones.

Get a notebook – or your planner – and write down all the prompts you liked the best, then see how many you have. You can even break them down into 'easy, quick prompts' that you could do on a daily basis, and other prompts that take longer or require more effort, which you could perhaps do every week or every month.

Then, put each of these favourite prompts into your calendar or diary for the year ahead (or several months, or however long you want) and make sure you do them. Repetition equals rewards, as I say in my *Write Your Life* book, and the more you repeat these prompts, the more effective they will be.

Remember – I created the free Write Your Year planner for this very purpose! (Get it at www.jessicagracecoleman.com/planner).

You can now continue with the Write Your Year prompts that work for you, without having to constantly refer back to this book.

You can even get your friends or family in on the action, asking them to join you in completing certain prompts throughout the year. Just make sure you plan the date ahead and get it scheduled in everyone's calendar, otherwise it probably won't happen. Repetition equals rewards and scheduling equals results!

365.

Write a journal entry, describing exactly how you feel in this moment. Ask yourself the following questions:

- Are you happy right now?

- Do you feel more fulfilled than you did a year ago?

- What's the biggest issue or most pressing concern in your life right now?

- Have you changed anything about yourself over the past year?

- Have you made any improvements to your life in terms of your job, house, relationship, fitness, or health?

- What one word would you use to describe your emotional state in this moment?

Be as honest as possible. You don't have to show this to anyone else. Then compare your answers to those for prompt number one, right back at the start of your Write Your Year journey. What have you learnt? How have you changed? How much have you grown as a person? What do the differences in your answers tell you about how much you've achieved over the past 12 months?

CONCLUSION

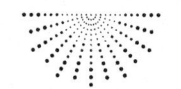

Congratulations, you've made it to the end!

Even if you've only done a handful of the prompts in this book, I applaud you. It's not easy trying something new, and it definitely isn't easy stepping outside your comfort zone. But you did it – way to go!

If you haven't already downloaded your free planner, get on it now (www.jessicagracecoleman.com/planner) to make the most of the prompts in this book, and hey, why not challenge one of your friends to try some of these prompts themselves (or even make up some of your own)? Pay it forward, spread the love, and help someone else step out of their comfort zone to achieve something awesome. If you've tried these prompts and had some wins, you'll know that it can be a true game changer in terms of the way you live your life.

Finally, if you've enjoyed this book, I would really appreciate it if you could please take a moment to write a review on Amazon. Reviews make ALL the difference for authors, and the more reviews this book gets, the more people the Write Your Life message will be able to reach. Thank you!

I hope you've had a brilliant time writing the past year, and I hope you take some of the lessons learnt from this book with you into the future.

So, what are you waiting for? Go ahead and write your year – and your life!

ABOUT THE AUTHOR

Hi, my name's Jess, and I'm a word nerd. I'm also a writing, editing, country music-loving self-proclaimed introvertpreneur with a passion for helping people change their lives through writing.

I love reading, I love writing, I love the rhythm of words when I'm typing them on my computer or reading them out loud from one of my favourite books. I love how powerful words are, and how – in the right context and with the right intentions – they can literally change the world.

I've been writing for as long as I can remember, but since 2014 I've made my full-time living from words, and I hope to continue doing so for a long time to come. In the past I've run online writing competitions, founded my own music zine, and worked for a copywriting agency where I wrote business blogs, articles, brochures, and more. Now I'm a proofreader, editor, and ghostwriter over at my own business, Coleman Editing, as well as the founder of Flip The Script Travel Transformation Services (www.traveltransformationcoach.com) and the host of The Travel Transformation Podcast.

During my time at Coleman Editing I've worked on hundreds of novels, non-fiction books, short stories, essays, articles, and poems. I've self-published nine of my own books, and my work has appeared in various collections and anthologies. I've gone on several writing retreats both in my home country of England and abroad, including a two-month writing residency on the stunning Thai island of Koh Samui. When travelling, I've dragged my travel partners to famous literary locations (and to the houses of famous authors) all over the world. I think it's fair to say, I'm kind of into writing.

For over two years I suffered from agonising and debilitating back pain caused by sitting down at a desk and working long hours. For months at a time I could barely even leave the house (way before the pandemic!), which affected me mentally as well as physically. After getting over the moping phase of what I thought of as my 'house arrest', I used the extra time to set up jessicagracecoleman.com and to write my first self-development book, *Write Your Life: The Ultimate Life Hack For Achieving Your Dreams*.

When I started my new venture I knew I wanted to make it a purpose-driven business. So, not only do we have a purpose of helping as many people as possible with both their writing and their lives, but we also want to give back as much as possible. As many of us are writers (of one kind or another) here, I've chosen two wonderful organisations to work with that relate to reading and writing. Firstly, 10% of the profits we make from the *Write Your Life* book are donated to Dolly Parton's Imagination Library – which, every month, sends out free books to children aged 0-5 in the US, UK, and several other countries. And, secondly, for every person who signs up to my Flip The Script Academy, we'll plant a tree through One Tree Planted.

You can find out more about me at my website, www.jessicagracecoleman.com, and you can follow me on Instagram @traveltransformationcoach.

OTHER BOOKS BY JESSICA GRACE COLEMAN

Also Available by Jessica Grace Coleman

Little Forest Series

The Former World

Memento Mori

The Exalted

Carnival Masquerade

The Gloaming

The Downfall Trilogy

The Downfall

Short Story Collections

Grown By The Wicked Moon

Non-Fiction

Intentional Travel Transformation: Boost Your Confidence, Conquer Your Fears & Finally Become The Person You've Always Wanted To Be

Write Your Life: The Ultimate Life Hack For Achieving Your Dreams

Creative Ways To Start Creative Writing

CONNECT WITH JESS

Email

author@jessicagracecoleman.com

Website

www.jessicagracecoleman.com

Instagram

@traveltransformationcoach

Facebook

@traveltransformationcoach

Sign up to Jessica Grace Coleman's mailing list at www.jessicagracecoleman.com for freebies, competitions, inspiration, and news about all of Jessica's new releases.

JOIN OUR INSTA CHALLENGE

I love to know when my readers are actually sitting down and doing the work, so I have a challenge for you. Post a pic of yourself with the *Write Your Year* book and then tag me in it (@traveltransformationcoach), along with the following three hashtags:

#writeyouryearpromptbook

#writeyourlifemethod

#imawriteyourlifer

If you're feeling brave enough, include some of the writing you're doing as part of the exercises in the caption, or describe some of your wins. I'll share it on my profile, and I'll also enter you into a draw to win a signed copy of the book along with some other Write Your Life goodies.

If you DM me with any wins you've had because of the Write Your Life Method, I'll also give you a shout-out on my Insta account!

INTRO TO WRITE YOUR LIFE

And now, here's a little freebie for you – the complete intro to my book, Write Your Life: The Ultimate Life Hack For Achieving Your Dreams.

> "Life isn't about finding yourself. Life is about creating yourself"
>
> — GEORGE BERNARD SHAW

Do you want to change your life? Change your path? Change your story? What if I told you that, at any time and for any reason, you could sit down and completely rewrite your story? Would you do it?

We are the authors of our own lives, but many of us never even pick up the pen; we just let life happen to us without ever deciding what we really, truly want – and without putting a plan into action so we can accomplish our goals and achieve our wildest dreams. Instead we just go with the flow, letting other people write our stories for us. We let them dictate our purpose in life, telling us what we should and shouldn't be doing. Fortunately, it doesn't have to be that way. Life is what you make it. Life is what you *write* it to be. And you can write whatever you want.

We have just one incredibly short life on this earth, but many of us never find our purpose, the reason we were put here on this planet. Well, what if I told you that your 'reason' for being here – your ultimate purpose – isn't some ethereal thing blowing in the wind that you're never quite able to catch, but is actually something you choose and create for yourself? We may not know the big purpose behind the existence of humankind, but we can certainly figure out our own individual purposes, and perhaps that's enough. Perhaps that's everything.

Do you wake up every morning less than enthused about getting up and starting your day? Do you wish there was something more? Something else? Something better? Surely there must be more to life than toiling away at a job you hate for 40 or 50 years until you retire? Surely there must be more than living paycheque to paycheque, always worrying about money or security? Surely this constant battle is not the point of life – this 'meaning' we're all meant to be searching for? *Surely* that's not our 'purpose'?

Putting it bluntly, what would be the point of that? I'm sure that whoever or whatever created this wonderful, beautiful, magnificent planet didn't have this hideous stressful struggle in mind for the people who live here. Why create this amazing world only to fill it with miserable, unfulfilled human beings just trying to make it through the day?

* * *

Find your purpose – and if you can't, create it!

If you feel this way, you're not alone. It's how many people feel all around the world, and it's how I felt up until around 2014, when I started making a series of life-changing decisions that led me to this point, right now, when I'm writing the introduction to a book I believe can help hundreds of thousands of people change the way they think, transform the way they look at their lives, and help them achieve the dreams they've been 'chasing' for years. That's *my* purpose, *my* meaning, and I got here not by coincidence or by some kind of miracle, but through endless hours of research, studying, and working to change my perspective on my past, my present, and – most importantly – my future. It's taken me years and years to get here and to gain clarity on what I really want, but with the help of this book you can get there far quicker – and with the Write Your Life Method, you'll even have fun along the way. You just need to be willing to think outside the box, take a step or two outside your comfort zone, and do the specific writing exercises and action steps I've laid out in the following chapters.

It might seem a little weird and even a little crazy at first, but what's the point in life if we don't get a little weird and crazy every now and then? Our life is our own to live, but even more importantly, it's our own to design. And I'm not going to design mine to be mundane, predictable, and uninteresting – who would? – I'm going to design mine to be as amazing as I can make it. What's the point in aiming for anything less? Some people might say it's too hard or too difficult, and yes, that's true – stepping outside your comfort zone and working towards your dreams *is* hard. But so is spending your entire life slogging away for a few pennies here and there and hating the existence you've created for yourself. Choose your 'hard'. I know which one I prefer.

If you don't know who I am, my name's Jess, I live in Staffordshire in the English countryside, and I'm a wordaholic. I'm also a writing, editing, country music-loving self-proclaimed introvertpreneur with a passion for helping people change their lives through writing.

I love reading, I love writing, I love the rhythm of words when I'm typing them on my computer or reading them out loud from one of my favourite books... yes, I'm a word nerd. I love how powerful words are, and how – in the right context and with the right intentions – they can literally change the world.

I've been writing for as long as I can remember, but since 2014 I've made my full-time living from words, and I hope to continue doing so for a long time to come. In the past I've run online writing competitions, founded my own music zine, and worked for a copywriting agency where I wrote business blogs, articles, brochures, and more. Now I'm a proofreader, editor, and ghostwriter over at my own business, Coleman Editing, as well as the founder of Flip The Script Travel Transformation Services (www.traveltransformationcoach.com).

Personally, I know exactly what it's like to wake up every morning dreading the day ahead, as I used to be stuck in a dead-end job... or, more accurately, a long string of dead-end jobs. I tried many different occupations over the years – canal boat cleaner, chambermaid, call centre operative, data entry clerk, administrator, administrative assistant, shop assistant, cinema worker, cinema team manager, and more – before I realised I needed to make a more radical change in my life. I was working minimum wage jobs because I didn't think I deserved to earn any more. I didn't think someone like me – a quiet, reserved introvert who found it difficult to speak up in pretty much any situation – could ever do more with my life than work long, crappy hours for someone else, doing menial or basic tasks. So I didn't even try to do anything else.

These limiting beliefs held me back for years, but eventually I reached breaking point. I'd had enough. I didn't want to do it anymore – I *couldn't* do it anymore. I needed to take action, and not just in the form of applying for yet another low-paid job that had nothing to do with my interests or dreams. Instead of looking for meaning and purpose in a ready-made role, I needed to create that role for myself, create my *purpose* for myself. It was going to take guts, but even though I was terrified, I knew I had to do it. I didn't have any other option.

Life is so ridiculously short and I didn't want to spend the few years I had on this earth hating my job or waking up every day filled with a deep foreboding feeling. That doesn't help me, and it certainly doesn't allow me to help anyone else. I knew that if I was to have any chance of living an exciting, fulfilling life, I had to push myself right out of my little comfort zone and into the strange and wonderful land of uncertainty, instability, and pure, unadulterated, wonderful fear. So that's exactly what I did.

It was during a family holiday to Majorca that I made the decision to quit my low-paid job and start my own business. I'd had such a nice time in the sun, far away from work, but the whole time I was there I'd felt this underlying dread knowing that as soon as I got back to the UK, I'd have to go back to a job I hated with all my heart. Surely that heart could be put to better use elsewhere?

At this point I was 27 years old, I was living with one of my best friends in a share house in my hometown, and I was working part-time as a team leader at the local cinema while doing freelance copywriting gigs on the side. On the last day of that holiday, as I sat in the gorgeous Spanish sun looking out at the beautiful blue water, I brought up the subject with my brother, who has run his own businesses for most of his working life.

Prior to coming on the holiday I'd tried running a Facebook ad asking if anyone needed an editor, and from that ad I'd got a couple of clients and had made quite a good profit (this was back when Facebook ads were only a few years old, and were pretty simple to use). Because of this initial return on investment, my brother encouraged me to go after what I wanted and to make a living doing what I loved – writing. I knew I didn't need 'permission' from anyone to do this, but it certainly helped knowing that someone else thought I was capable of doing it.

I wrestled with this decision as we headed back to England – but in all honesty I'd already made up my mind – and on my first shift back I handed in my notice. I started my own proofreading, editing, and ghostwriting business right then, as well as continuing to self-publish my own novels and non-fiction books. I never looked back.

It took a while to get things right and for everything to click, but now I get up excited for the day ahead, knowing that I don't have to suffer through a long commute to get to work, knowing that I don't have a boss to please or endless pointless meetings to attend, and knowing that I get to write my life the way *I* want to write it… every single day. I used to dream of working for myself, and now I get to live that dream. But it's better than that – better than I could possibly have ever imagined – as now I also get to help others achieve *their* dreams, whether that dream is writing their first ever book or changing their life through writing.

That is my purpose, the meaning I'd been searching for. And I created it myself.

* * *

Making the most of lockdown

Life is all about making the most of the time we have, something that's very much on my mind – and everyone else's – as I write these words. I came up with the idea for this book when the 2020 Coronavirus pandemic started locking down several countries, and by the time I'd planned it and started writing, the UK was in full on lockdown. We were only allowed to leave the house for essential things like shopping for food or for medical needs, and for one walk a day. Key workers could obviously still go to work (and what heroes they are), but the majority of us – if we could – had to work from home. If you were on the 'vulnerable' list, you were told not to leave the house at all if you could help it.

I am fortunate enough to work from home anyway, and due to some back problems I'd been having for the previous year or so I'd pretty much been housebound for ten months (off and on) before the pandemic hit, so you could say I'd been in training for it.

Pretty early on in the lockdown, my self-employed work (writing, editing, and proofreading) started drying up, and realising that the lockdown was likely to continue for several months, I knew I had a decision to make. I could hustle myself to death trying to get editing clients to keep my current business afloat (which wouldn't have been good for my health), I could give up and veg out for the remainder of the quarantine (which wouldn't have been good for my health or my bank account), or I could do something positive that would help people and give them some form of purpose during this terrifying time.

I chose the latter. I wrote this book. I also set up my new website, took two online business courses, read as many business and self-development books as I could, and listened to as many informative and uplifting podcasts as possible – and, as I couldn't physically sit down, or even stand up for some of that time due to my back injury, I did all of that (plus my day job of running my editing business) while lying down. It was a pain in the ass – literally. And yes, while the whole COVID-19 nightmare was scary and while I worried for my friends and family, instead of spiralling out and losing the plot I chose to look at things from another perspective. I had all this extra time (not having as much work on, not being able to go out or even move much), and I was determined to make the most of it.

It's all about shifting your mindset, looking at things from a different angle, and opening your mind up to new possibilities. At the start of the lockdown I knew exactly what I wanted to do, so I set the intention, took the necessary action, and achieved my goal, using several of the tips and techniques featured in this book. And that's exactly what you can do too. It may not be easy, but it is that simple.

* * *

What you'll get out of the Write Your Life Method

You may have several objectives in mind as you're reading this book – and subsequently when you're doing the exercises and putting the method into action – and that's fine. There are so many things you can get out of going through the assignments in these pages. For instance, this book can help you:

• Make minor and major life decisions

• Come to terms with certain things in your past and get closure on events, people, and anything else you've been holding onto, whether you knew you were holding onto them or not

- See how the things you've done in the past (or the things that have happened to you) have shaped you into the awesome person you are today, and be grateful for them

- Identify the 'ambitions' you have for your dream life, and whittle them down to your Top Three Dreams that you can start taking action on today

- Come up with a clear, precise Ultimate Dream Blueprint to help you achieve your goals and attain your dream life

- End up with your very own Write Your Life Story, a fictionalised account of you and your journey that will encourage you on your path to achieving your dreams

- If you wish, turn your finished Write Your Life Story into a physical paperback and flick through it whenever you need to remind yourself how amazing you are for completing this book, or whenever you need to review your Ultimate Dream Blueprint.

* * *

Creativity as therapy

I'm not a therapist, but I've seen first-hand how writing can help people come to terms with their pasts, appreciate their present, and visualise a bright, exciting future for themselves. We talk about 'pouring our heart out' in therapy, and that's exactly what we do with writing – just with a pen, or the keys on our keyboard. Whether it's fiction or autobiography, the very act of writing things down can help us release certain feelings and emotions we've been holding onto, letting it all out instead of keeping everything bottled up inside. Why else do we keep diaries? Why else do people journal or blog about their personal lives?

The act of writing can also help us shift both our mindset and our energy. If you spend all day on a computer, doing a stressful job, looking after kids, or whatever else you do, sitting down in a quiet space and writing down your thoughts and feelings can be the energy shift you need in order to de-stress and reflect. Creativity is a big part of therapy – just think of art therapy, music therapy, dance therapy – and writing is no different. It gives you the chance to express yourself in ways you might not be able to otherwise, and it can help us gain a real sense of self, while also gaining clarity about our lives. This book uses writing therapy techniques but comes at them from a different angle… hopefully one that is even more creative and a whole load of fun.

* * *

Looking at life from a novel perspective

When you're reading a book, or watching a TV show or a movie, do you sometimes find yourself rolling your eyes at the page, or shouting at the screen, because the main character's about to do something immensely stupid? Or because you can tell what's about to happen? Or because you think you could have written it better yourself? We all do it, and we always know what's best for the characters we're reading about or watching on screen. Don't go down into that dark basement alone… don't go into the house where the killer is without waiting for backup… don't date the handsome yet clearly evil guy while the good-hearted scruffy country dude waits in the wings… I'm sure some of us do it with our friends and family members too. We want to blurt out, 'Why are you dating that girl when she's really mean to you?' or 'Why are you staying in that job when it's making you so miserable?' or 'What will it take to make you two see you're perfect for each other?'

If we can do this so easily with the lives of other people – whether they be characters in a book or our own friends – why can't we do it with our own lives? Why can't we take a step back, look at what's happening as though it were happening in a novel, and give ourselves the same advice we give fictional people on a regular basis? Why can't we look at our own situations – such as when we have an important decision to make – and see it from an outsider's perspective? As if we were reading about an epic romance story? Or a coming-of-age narrative? Or a redemption story? Perhaps it's a rags-to-riches tale, or a story about a timid girl who blossoms into an awesome powerhouse businesswoman? Or better yet, as if we were *writing* our story ourselves, which is what we should be doing anyway, every single day of our lives?

Too many people make the mistake of just letting life happen to them, without even realising *they* have the power to write the next chapter, the next page, the next sentence – if only they'd bother to pick up the pen.

Fiction always includes conflict of some kind, but it also includes heroes and heroines, people who overcome terrible obstacles and who escape from horrific circumstances to come out triumphantly on the other side, having learned the necessary lessons and grown in all kinds of ways to become the person they were always meant to be. And what is fiction if not a reflection of life?

This is about waking up tomorrow, looking at that fresh, blank page, and deciding to take control – deciding to be the author of your own life. After all, isn't that what's supposed to happen? We have one life on this earth (as far as I know), and *we* should be the ones to write our own stories – not our family, not our friends, not our bosses or our peers or anyone else. *Us*.

You can complete the exercises in this book in many different ways. As a lot of it will be deeply personal, you might wish to do this alone and not have anyone else read through your answers, and that's absolutely fine. Alternatively, you might want to gather a group of close friends and work through this book and the exercises together. This can actually be pretty fun, and you might learn something about your friends that brings you even closer together.

Or you might wish to work through the exercises alone, then ask for feedback from a third party – either someone you trust, or a complete stranger (both will have different and valuable perspectives), allowing you to see your life from yet more angles.

Believe me, this can be a game-changer. Getting a potential reader's perspective on a 'work in progress' is always fascinating and eye-opening, giving you things to think about that you might not have ever considered before – so just think how powerful this could be when *you're* the main character. I bet the feedback you receive could change the way you think about, well, pretty much anything. Going forward, it will also allow you to view situations from entirely new perspectives. There's no right or wrong way to do this, but if you do the exercises and stick with it, you will see results.

And, as a special gift to all my Write Your Life students, I've created a completely free *Write Your Life Workbook*, which is full of worksheets you can print off and fill in as you go through the book and complete the exercises. I highly recommend you print off a copy and have it to hand as you work your way through the chapters – get it at www.jessicagracecoleman.com/writeyourlife.

***

Going above thirty miles an hour

If you're already into self-development and personal growth there's a good chance you've read *The Big Leap* by Gay Hendricks (and if you haven't, I highly recommend it). It's all about conquering fear and finding your 'zone of genius', but there's one bit that really stood out to me, an excellent example of limiting beliefs and how it takes just one moment of bravery – and the willingness to step outside your comfort zone – to achieve something truly wonderful:

"In the early days of the steam-powered train, learned scientists urged capping the speed at thirty miles per hour because they believed that the human body exploded at speeds greater than that. Finally, some brave people risked going beyond that limiting belief and found that they did not explode" – Gay Hendricks, *The Big Leap*.

Crazy, right? It's even crazier when you know that some people believed going above 50 miles an hour on a train would cause women's uteruses to fly out of their bodies!

Imagine if no one had ever dared going above 30 miles an hour because they were sure they were going to die? Imagine if no one had set sail to explore the world because they were too scared of getting to the 'end' and falling off? Imagine if no one had ever invented chocolate because they were worried it would be too unhealthy? Truly inconceivable.

Now imagine you were one of those brave souls who went above 30 miles an hour. It would take just one moment, one decision, one single step outside your comfort zone, and you'd be able to achieve something incredible.

So, are you ready to get on that train and start increasing your speed? Are you ready to start exploring your world with all its exciting possibilities? Are you ready to eat that delicious chocolate, and really enjoy it (because some things in life are truly sweet, if only we let ourselves go after them)? If you are, let's get to it. And the good thing is, you're not going to explode – that's a Write Your Life guarantee.

Printed in Great Britain
by Amazon